THE ULTIMATE SURVIVAL GUIDE TO LIFE,
STRESS, FINANCE & EVERYTHING IN BETWEEN

MORE THAN OKAY-ISH

SARA SIDWELL &
MICHELLE RICCETTO

Publisher: WOXY Press LLC, 6650 Rivers Avenue, North Charleston, SC 29406

ISBN Hardback: 979-8-9875797-5-6

ISBN Paperback: 979-8-9875797-6-3

ISBN eBook: 979-8-9875797-7-0

Disclaimer Notice:

Please note that the information contained within this document is for educational and entertainment purposes only. All effort has been executed to present accurate, up-to-date, reliable, and complete information. No warranties of any kind are declared or implied. Readers acknowledge that the author is not engaged in the rendering of legal, financial, medical, or professional advice. The content within this book has been derived from various sources. Please consult a licensed professional before attempting any techniques outlined in this book.

This book was previously released under the title *How To Get Your Shift (replace 'if' with *) Together.* Due to censorship, the new title, *More Than Okay-ish,* was selected, and the book was republished with an updated To My Dear Readers and Preface.

This book is based on real events and the real lives of both authors, but minor details have been changed for privacy's sake.

Table of Contents

Dedications

To everyone who feels lost and overwhelmed trying to get ahead on the hamster wheel of life. This book is for you.

And to the zoo in my house, thank you for the frequent interruptions that keep me sane.

–Sara

To every person in my life that showed me love, empathy, and kindness as I healed my deepest wounds and found my way out of the darkness, thank you.

Looking at you, Kav & Erin. Without you both, I would not be where I am now, standing in my own strength and power. Thank you.

Sara, thank you for taking a chance on me. You've inspired me beyond words (including all these ones).

And to my muse, you ignite my soul. I'm sorry it took me so long to figure that out.

– Michelle

To my dear readers

"You may encounter many defeats, but you must not be defeated. In fact, it may be necessary to encounter the defeats, so you can know who you are, what you can rise from, how you can still come out of it."

— *Maya Angelou*

Welcome to my book, where we'll say the quiet parts out loud. As a writer, I prefer not to delicately dance around blunt truths we all must learn to survive and thrive in this modern world. So, fair warning, from here on, no filters. Just straight talk.

Let's start by acknowledging that life can be a full-on nightmare. One you can't seem to wake up from if you haven't developed the skills, gained the knowledge, or gotten the right support to help yourself break free from life's sometimes soul-sucking rinse-and-repeat cycles.

But it can also be where you encounter moments of awe and wonder that transcend the ordinary. Moments where you marvel at the vastness and beauty surrounding you or experience the electric energy of new ideas and connections.

We all experience a life full of peaks and valleys, highs and lows, ups and downs. Regardless of your success rate on your bucket list, this doesn't mean you will have smooth sailing ahead—or vice versa. Expect to get bumped around. If you're not, I suggest you're probably not challenging yourself enough to live up to your potential.

The opposite is true as well. For those of us who have faced traumas and hardships that most will never understand, please know that you are not confined to that trajectory. You, too, as the opening quote says, can rise.

Understand that within each of us is more strength, grit, and determination than you can imagine. Many of us haven't even been close to testing our limits. You were made to do hard things, and within you is the capacity for so much more than you allow yourself to believe or maybe even dare to dream.

Yes, there will always be days when life devolves into an absolute shitshow testing your resolve. You are allowed to have moments of doubt, bad days, and what-in-the-fuck-am-I-doing days. On those days, self-care, bravery, and how you show up for yourself will matter most.

Consider how you showed up for yourself in front of the mirror this morning. What did your inner conversation sound like? It is essential to be cognizant that your reflection holds far more than who you are now and the sum of your past.

I'd like you to embrace the idea that your reflection also offers a glimpse of a future new version of you, waiting to be unleashed. One that only needs the right encouragement, support, and skills to set it free. And reading this book is an important first step in your personal journey to doing just that.

You have the power to change your inner conversation so that it serves as a reminder for you to take every day as an opportunity to improve, grow, and develop your authenticity. To be relentless in pursuing self-discovery and not stop until you are the person you have always wanted to be.

Whether you're an anxious soul, hesitant to make any changes, or a determined individual driven and ready to make big changes, there's no better time to do it than now.

Are you ready to have an intentional life that's *More Than Okay-ish*?

–Sara

Starting today...

I will stop letting my past define me.

I will no longer accept the status quo.

I will stop all negative self-talk.

I will stop telling myself I missed my chance.

I will stop telling myself I'm not good enough.

I will stop telling myself I can't get ahead.

I will stop telling myself I'm not smart enough.

I will stop telling myself success is only for others.

I will stop telling myself I'm too old or young to make it.

I give myself permission to let all that shit go.

I'm changing the narrative.

What I want matters—I matter.

I am unstoppable.

I am resilient and strong.

I am ready to live a life that's more than just okay.

—Sara Sidwell

Preface

"Courage is not having the strength to go on; it is going on when you don't have the strength."

— *Teddy Roosevelt*

Glamour < grit.

If you are reading this book because you are looking for help breaking free from everything holding you back and creating a new life full of authenticity and endless possibilities, you are exactly for whom this book was written.

Here, you'll learn valuable skills and tips often not taught by parents, teachers, or professors that you'll need to help break free from the daily rinse-and-repeat cycles that leave you feeling stuck with your ideals, actions, and dreams out of alignment.

Cumulative chapters supported by easy-to-follow exercises are specifically designed to help you get going. Along the way, you'll find hard-earned insights, blunt truths, inspiration, and hopefully some validation that it's not just you—life really is fucking hard.

Instead of false promises, this book will call it like it is. You'll gain the necessary knowledge to build a solid foundation to support and organize your ambitions, enable you to chase your dreams, and empower you to reach your life's personal and financial goals. You will learn how to disconnect from external pressures and influences and keep the focus on you, where it matters most.

The solid foundation you'll create will help keep you grounded, grateful, and mindful of who you are and where you've been, and find appreciation for you and your life right now. So, you stay authentic as you create and grow.

While change takes time and patience, this book does not. It's deliberately written to be more of a bite-sized, quick-access manual that you can use to jumpstart your self-development, build quick momentum to take those next steps or flip through when you need a push or a reminder. I've skipped the fluff, the long-winded stories, most of which are humble bragging, and instead, get to the point in a no-nonsense, straightforward, beginner-friendly way.

As someone who has struggled with crippling anxiety and panic attacks, I understand the gravity that mental health has on every aspect of our lives. I brought on Michelle Riccetto to co-author the book with me to blend in her candor and perspective as a mental health advocate and survivor of child abuse, intimate partner abuse, and sexual-based violence—as well as someone navigating life with PTSD and ADHD. Her honesty about her experiences across her social media platforms portrays a woman with a visceral and unrelenting drive to reduce stigmas and normalize conversations regarding mental health. I wanted to channel that energy into this book, as I felt it would resonate with others on their own healing journey reading this.

We are both testaments to the enduring resilience that lives within each of us—living proof on the value of the information shared within these pages.

Let's get started.

–Sara & Michelle

Chapter 1:

Welcome to the jungle.

"Change will not come if we wait for some other person or some other time. We are the ones we've been waiting for. We are the change that we seek."

— Barack Obama

How I got here...

My love of music goes back to my earliest memories. As a little girl, I fondly remember singing along with my mother as she played the piano. In elementary school, this love of music prompted me to join the school band, where I played multiple instruments—the flute, piccolo, clarinet, and even the alto and tenor saxophones.

Music offered me more than just a hobby; it was both a passion and refuge for me. It could both ignite my soul and soothe it. Music and books were my safe space in an otherwise unhappy childhood. Within their creative refuge, my mind was able to escape the abuse, violence, neglect, and fear to survive another day in a world where safety and love eluded me.

During high school, I was exposed to heavy metal rock music for the first time. I went to a Judas Priest & Iron Maiden concert with my friends at Madison Square Garden. More than just a night out, this event would be pivotal for me in many ways. I felt alive again with the energy of the music, the crowd—of New York City. I felt *something* again. And I felt like I wasn't alone anymore.

This powerful music spoke to me during a difficult time of my life and provided a much-needed outlet. Not only was I navigating the hellscape of being a teenager in their formative years, but I was going through major life transitions and emerging from the survival mode the abuse and trauma forced me into.

It was also during this time that Guns n' Roses released "Welcome to the Jungle." The intense and emotionally charged vocals of Axl Rose, with the raw energy of their powerful guitar riffs, not only perfectly captured the era of rock known for its leather, long hair, and rebellion, but it also ignited my creative spark. One that had laid dormant so I could focus on just trying to survive.

So, with this new energy and passion, I went and bought a bass guitar and taught myself how to play by ear. Within six months, I joined an all-female heavy metal band.

Hanging out with the band, practicing, and writing songs consumed my life. I wrote instrumentals and song lyrics and sang backup vocals on top of playing bass. I found myself eagerly devoting hours upon hours to songwriting. Staying up late at night and hurriedly scribbling on napkins and receipts whenever an idea or lyric came to me — the band and our music were my everything. I felt seen, supported, and free to express myself without judgement. At the time, like many teenagers and young adults before me and after, I knew that I wanted to do this for the rest of my life.

I continued to pursue my career in music for years, often broke, but overall, I was happy doing what I loved. As the years progressed, I married a wonderful man and my best friend, and together we had a beautiful daughter. But even her birth did not stop my dream of making it big in the music industry. At least, not right away.

During the first year of motherhood, I reveled in being both a mother and a musician. My daughter brought new levels of energy and inspiration to my creativity and expression. While being on the road presented a plethora of challenges for a young family, I was married to a great man and father that supported my ambitions. The music career I always dreamed of really did seem possible.

But then sometimes life throws you a curveball and really fucks everything up.

Though I did end up divorcing my husband, that would not be the ol' curveball. My husband and I were really good at being best friends. We built a beautiful and loving family but lacked the romantic love and connection we both wanted from a spouse. We remained a family unit, best friends, and fully involved in each other's lives. The curveball would come in the form of cancer. My daughter and I would lose her father and my best friend at a young age. We were on our own.

The music industry is a tough gamble and a fickle business, even without the added challenge of being a single mother. Splitting my time between trying to be a good mom and being a productive member of the band proved to be too much. I lived in a constant state of exhaustion and financial stress — always waiting for the other shoe to drop. I knew that to support my family, I was going to have to make a hard choice.

After everything I'd been through, I knew my daughter's well-being and providing her with a healthy, stable home life came first. By the sheer act of having children, we make the commitment to putting their needs and best interests first — even if it means sacrificing something significant on our end.

At the time, it felt like I had to let my dream of becoming a successful musician end to ensure my baby girl's well-being. As far as I knew, I would never reach for that dream again. But with my determination to do right by her, I began looking for other ways to make a living that provided a better family life and were more sustainable and conducive to raising a child.

Stability, that elusive minx.

Fueled by the burning need to secure a new source of income, I hung up my leather jacket and went back to school part-time, graduating with a degree in finance and psychology.

Finance is not known for sparking late-night debates or as an expressive outlet for impassioned souls. Unlikely, you'd get invited to a hipster coffee shop or bar to listen to a tortured CFA or financial analyst funnel their rage and rebellion on commodity pricing or estate planning into slam poetry or an original acoustic number. But even to my surprise, I liked finance and discovered another side to myself and another way to show the world who I was—only now as a (badass) businesswoman. Gone were my days of ripped jeans and studded belts; I was about to be an office warrior with cardigans.

With a BS degree in hand and a strong sense of responsibility for my daughter, I began my search for a position that would financially provide for my little family, meet our immediate needs, and would **not** drain the life out of me every day. Take care of the necessities. Stop being broke. Not hate my job with a fiery passion. Rinse and repeat.

It took some time, but I landed a position at a small corporation with a balanced work/life culture full of genuinely kind people. It didn't pay overly well at the start, but it came with good benefits, and I liked the work. Moreover, it satiated my desire for income stability.

In today's world of philosophy by meme or wisdom by influencer, your career trajectory or life's path is often boiled down to some nonsensical "poetic" line about chasing your bliss. What is lacking in these images of sunsets and fields of wildflowers with perfectly placed coffee mugs is anything remotely related to financial stability.

Not having enough to meet your basic needs is an unbearable struggle. I know. I've been there. I've slept in the back of my car. Finding a way to provide for yourself and anyone that relies on you is a major accomplishment. Chasing your "bliss" is a privilege that not everyone has because meeting your basic needs trumps any warm hug you feel in your soul when you paint the ocean or photograph cats.

But that also doesn't mean you need to be relegated to some soul-crushing cubicle farm, behind a register, or on a construction site doing work that makes one of those COVID nasal swab tests feel like a spa weekend just because they pay well and there's opportunity. This isn't a zero-sum game.

Allow yourself to discover more interests. Then pursue a career that offers both financial stability and growth in addition to something that piques your interests. I never once thought when I was on the road and getting the adrenaline rushes from performing in front of an audience that one day, I would be a corporate analyst.

But life is weird, and I soon learned that I am allowed to be more than just a musician. I am allowed to pursue more than just one type of passion, and my passions and pursuits can be in complete contradiction with one another. We don't need to fit into neat little boxes of cohesive identities.

At a young age, it was drilled into me that to be taken more seriously in the career world as a woman; I *had* to have a degree. Companies looked upon prospective employees more favorably if they had one, and for the most part, that remains true. So, like many others looking to make their way into a higher-paying position, I ensured I had that coveted degree and, along the way, discovered a lot about myself and other interests I never would have known otherwise.

Many people pursue higher education for no other reason than landing a job that leads to a lucrative position with good benefits to help mitigate personal costs and those associated with having a family — and there is nothing wrong with that. For many, work is just a means to fund and support their life's passions, such as having family, traveling the world, or creating a sense of safety and security in a close-knit community.

Being able to keep the bills paid consistently created a feeling of safety and contentment within me. I learned to ride out the downturns in the economy, rise above the occasional personality conflicts, and survive two rounds of layoffs—

more importantly, it taught me the benefits of perseverance. I had financial security goals from which I was unwilling to stray. But eventually, over time, my unwillingness to stray out of my carefully crafted comfort zone became suffocating, and my desire for financial security would directly impact my personal growth and my overall happiness.

The absolute audacity.

Change is inevitable. **It is also an asshole.** But if you're clutching your pearls right now because I've said another curse word, (1) you're in for a rough ride with this book, (2) don't watch anything on HBO, (3) I'll allow the great New England poet, Robert Frost, to sum up my sentiments a little more eloquently, "Nothing gold can stay" (Frost, 1923).

Like many of us on the precipice of change, I started noticing subtle changes beginning to surface, both at my workplace and within. They were slow at first, but then as they became more noticeable, I felt more anxiety and depression surface along with it. The company culture and my own satisfaction levels with my career were shifting, and change interferes with my ability to feel secure. So, I did what so many normal adults would do in this situation; I chose to ignore the warning signs in hopes they would resolve themselves.

They did not.

Even the best companies can evolve into ones that no longer fit into what you want or need, especially those that you started with early on in your career. Right after graduation, we're essentially all just baby deer, looking to find our footing and find a safe space that allows us to figure out the whole life big picture thing and grow stronger legs.

But with growth always comes change. After many years, the company I loved working for began to quickly outgrow its current configuration, both in terms of operations and people management—which is a fancy way of saying the little close-knit shop I worked for expanded into a large corporation and needed to level up in a very short period of time.

This rapid growth meant hiring and bringing in more people to keep up with demand and implementing new ways of doing business. What was once a unique and inclusive work culture where everyone worked openly together as one interactive team morphed into one becoming more siloed. Being separated and isolated from one another created a feeling of just being a number or name on a file. I kept to myself and holed up in my office, hanging on to my financial safety with emotionally tight fists.

With overall company restructuring, particularly the restructuring of human resources and a gross expansion of their authority, the autonomy we once had soon became a thing of the past. A bit of nostalgia we would sigh over while sharing coffee and eye rolls when we learned of yet another weekly HR overreach to limit the little autonomy we had left.

The most critical loss for me was the change in my job function. I worked my way up to becoming a senior-level analyst, collaborating with many different functional teams, being involved in exciting problem-solving and growth strategies, to then being relegated to data control and processing. I felt stagnant. The teamwork, the challenges, and the interesting problem-solving that sparked both the creative and logical sides of my brain just vanished.

Instead, I spent every hour of my workday, including my lunch time, staring at my computer monitor, processing data, and doing the same thing repeatedly.

And then my carefully crafted sense of safety and security was not just knocked over, but they set the damn thing on fire.

After 27 years of diligently working with the company, I was removed from the office I used since day one and moved into a cubicle. It was not just insulting, but it told me the nearly three decades of contributions and thousands of hours I had put into its success were not appreciated. It was worth nothing to my company. The loyalty only went one way.

So, I immediately flipped my desk over and told them, "Fuck you and fuck your cubicle," then bailed, giving high fives on my way out.

None of that happened. But I imagined it did oh so many times. My response in reality: I acted like a mature adult and stuck it out for a bit, ranting about the SHEER AUDACITY to my circle of close confidants to let out the brewing rage, hurt, disappointment, and frustration.

After cubicle-gate, the daily grind became even more unbearable, and I finally allowed myself to see the proverbial writing on the wall. I knew I would have to get out of my comfort zone and make a huge change. The thought of rocking the financial security boat was terrifying, but the reality of outgrowing my career was too blatant to ignore.

It took me months to gather up the courage to even consider stepping away from the security of that job. However, I made the mental leap to change it all after about six months. The mere act of making that decision would release a tremendous sense of urgency to start building my next chapter (pun intended). But I didn't know where or what the hell I was going to do next. I was back to being a wobbly baby deer, unsure and unfamiliar with how to use my legs or navigate the world around me.

I thought about going back to my music, but that thought was fleeting. Although creatively expressing myself ranks high on my values and what I want from my career, I realized in my few trips around the sun that financial freedom was more important to me and a significant player in my quest to find happiness once again. If I was going to break free and do this—really do this—I needed to up the stakes: more money and more freedom.

When I left my company, I was making a solid six-figure income and cushy bonuses along with great health benefits, nearly three months of paid time off a year, and a hefty 401(k) the company matched.

For me, leaving that position meant waaaaay more than just the nice paycheck. I knew that if illness or injury fell upon my family, I had us fully covered. I also knew I could afford the unplanned life hiccups, like unexpected car repairs, a flood in a basement, or a tutor for Spanish class. Financial security meant I could always meet our basic needs and provide for my family.

I told no one of my plans, not because I feared their judgment (okay, I did a bit), but because I didn't want their own projected fears of risk to negatively impact me and cause me to waver. I thought everyone would think I was utterly insane to leave such financial stability and security to chase greener pastures. And for some, it is. But I needed more.

Gold-plated liars.

Ever heard the saying that a conversation can change your life? For me, this life-changing conversation occurred on a routine evening with my daughter. She randomly popped off that I should start a drop shipping company. Of course, I had no idea what in the ever-living hell she was talking about, but I value her ideas, and I decided to investigate.

I did a *lot* of online research on starting up my own business, including spending hours and hours each day on the likes of TikTok and YouTube. Before I quit my job, I even spent my lunches at work picking up where I left off the night before. Starting my own business felt right, but what kind of business and approach remained elusive.

Before my ex-husband and I parted ways, I had helped him establish what became a midsized service company in heavy industry. With my hands-on experience building his business and the nearly three decades I spent rising the ranks in a corporate environment, I knew I was not a novice in the business world—but I still felt like I needed some guidance from "the pros."

Thankfully but not so thankfully, the social media algorithms immediately took notice of my new online viewing habits, and I soon became inundated with a flood of ads from influencers and entrepreneurs selling their expertise and surefire methods to make bank working for myself. They all seemed so confident, competent, and knowledgeable in their own way, but they were really hawking the same snake oil bullshit with a different veneer.

They all proclaimed to have *the* way. The way to sales, growth, financial freedom, passive income, free time, and prosperity in perpetuity. The more I dug into my research, the more confused I became and overwhelmed by the hyped-up sales ads, and I was soon stuck in analysis paralysis.

I opted to lessen the learning curve of starting my own online business by investing in some tools and education on the basics from a seller's perspective. I spent thousands of dollars (and countless hours) on what I thought was setting a solid foundation to minimize my risk and prepare me to launch successfully. In my ignorance, I thought I bought access to the tools necessary to understand this new-to-me market, but unfortunately, I didn't know what I didn't know.

The programs I purchased featured vibrant and encouraging "experts" that promised easy solutions and the reassurance a new entrepreneur is craving to hear. All you had to do was follow their foolproof guidance. You could avoid the hard work, the stress, and the gut punches of doing it alone—saving you a lot of time and money if you just took their course and listened to their success siren song. Because they obviously understood, and their likability, charisma, and what I now surmise is feigned empathy made me feel connected to these online personalities.

Initially, I opened a couple of online stores through the likes of Etsy and Shopify, platforms that felt less daunting and foreign to me now that I had taken courses that covered them. But the promise of all the answers to successfully master these e-commerce sites throughout my courses failed to prepare me for the amount of time and resources required to actually run the much longer list of tasks necessary to manage an online store.

Still, I kept shelling out money to find the answers, the secrets to success, with my sense of urgency driving me each time I entered my credit card number to find said answers.

Even when I became more careful about what courses I bought and paid for, I still spent hours attending online seminars and recordings. I kept trying to garner whatever nugget of information I could that would lead me to a life of wealth and freedom. I was hopeful and had already invested so much that I was certain I was only one pivotal learning experience away from it all clicking and just falling into place.

It never did fall into place with the online courses. I switched gears and almost purchased what I thought was the equivalent of "falling into place" with a turnkey e-commerce store. One of those done-for-you drop shipping stores designed and created just for you. They do everything for you, then hand you the keys to the kingdom, so to speak. Expensive, but at least the endless rotation of new courses would be over. I was exhausted and ready to pull the trigger. Let's just do this already.

Having already wasted a lot of money on courses, feeling frustrated and desperate to just move the fuck on, one night, I found myself with my finger on the submit payment button to buy an online store. Obviously, I was in the right mindset and headspace to make such an enormous decision. I would absolutely not regret making a large purchase in such a state of mental exhaustion and desperation for change.

Thankfully, my brain finally kicked into gear at the sight of the $35,000 price tag, and I snatched my hand back from an almost very reckless decision and closed the browser. I realized that in my frenzy to find my freedom and security once more, and from being caught up in the overload of sales content pressuring me to act, I was not in the best or clearest mindset.

Second, I had not done thorough enough research into the background of this company with whom I was about to risk my financial well-being. I, the queen of research, had not done my due diligence or even double-checked the company and was ready to make a serious gamble with some serious money.

But after my brain showed up, I started looking more closely at the videos, scrutinizing their surroundings, their clothing, and their presentation. Dread started to form in my stomach; something seemed off. I started trying to cross-reference them and other similar sites, and not one of them was validated independently. Sure, I could find 5-star reviews, but the ones I found screamed, "I am fake." I even discovered that one of the review websites was completely fake entirely. I almost handed these scam artists $35K and my credit card number.

Throughout this experience, part of me had always known it was too good to be true. That no one could honestly skip the hard work of creating and maintaining their own business and just jump straight to the success and lots of money part. These were lessons I had already learned throughout my life, both in setting up and supporting my husband's business and throughout my career as a corporate stiff. Anyone who runs a successful business will tell you the same thing: you must put in the work. But I wanted it to be true. So, I got caught up in all the hype and success of these online personalities, and because of this, I nearly jumped into a financially risky situation.

While I preach about taking ownership of your actions and your mistakes, it's also important to cut yourself some slack. We all make mistakes and can get swept up in the allure of finding an answer to all our problems, especially when they are packaged up nicely, constantly, and purposefully targeting you every day across digital platforms. These marketing campaigns are designed to lure you into spending your hard-earned money on their products and services with tactics meant to slither past our scrutiny and objections. They're in it for the sale, so it's important always to exercise caution and critically assess the claims being made and who is making them.

The machines are powerful, man.

Like me, you may have already paid the bridge troll—the price of earnestly trusting that the right service or product or Peruvian crystals offering you a better life will deliver... if only you spend a little on their magic cure. You may even be reflecting on it right now, perhaps feeling a bit embarrassed or maybe even beating yourself up for falling for a scam and wasting your time and money.

But, as I said before, cut yourself some slack.

You are not the first person, nor the last, that has fallen victim to an empty promise. Especially when these empty promises are part of a larger strategy to funnel endless content across your social channels, emails, and website ads until you start hitting the submit purchase button. Think of how many thousands of times you saw these attempts to sway you, and you said no. But the relentless nature of these targeted ads is based on powerful algorithms that track your online behavior —specifically to find methods of converting you into a customer.

Do you know what else is powerful? Learning from mistakes. Both from the ones you make and from the experience of others. I hope that by sharing some of mine, I can help you avoid a few and practice self-compassion when you do make mistakes.

My foray into e-commerce would prove to offer me more than just a few expensive lessons; it would also serve as a catalyst for my actual next steps.

Through all my e-commerce research, I also learned about writing books and self-publishing on platforms like Amazon. In the past, I always felt intimidated by the thought of rejection letters and navigating established publishing houses to find someone to give my writing a fair chance. My experience searching for the treasure map of success in e-commerce brought out an unexpected twist of fate.

And just like that, I was once again that teenager bursting with creativity and completely consumed by my desire for self-expression. Once again, I found passion through words, trading in song lyrics and heavy metal for books, and using this newfound inspiration to prepare five outlines for fiction books and another nonfiction book in addition to this one.

Michell and I both firmly believe that with the right support, validation, skills, and a little tough love, we all can transform our lives into something far more than just okay.

Chapter 2:

Everyone is mostly full of shit

on social media.

"The prettiest smiles hide the deepest secrets. The prettiest eyes have cried the most tears. And the kindest hearts have felt the most pain."

– Unknown

In modern culture, our commitment to showcasing our lives and careers as a shiny branded experience is nowhere more noticeable than on social media. This also reinforces the sentiments of my chapter title; social media is where the truth goes to die, and everyone is mostly full of shit.

There, the constant drumbeat from modern-day fortune tellers attempts to mesmerize and encourage you to find your passion or do what you love for only a couple of hours a day. Follow their example, and you, too, could be living in the most aesthetically pleasing home, with glass containers and labels for everything in your fridge and pantry.

Whatever the platform – TikTok, YouTube, Instagram, Snapchat, or Facebook for the older crowd – you see influencers and creators post enviable pictures and videos of exotic trips, glamourous nights out, lavish meals, and carefully crafted cocktails. Look at them; they figured out life and did it with a lot of cohesive style.

Even your friends and social network seemed to have found a way to snatch a taste of this luxe life. Everyone is having fun without you: smiling and dancing and laughing and eating figs and making latte art every morning in thick ceramic mugs with tidy home offices with impeccable views. They even have artisanal kale salads for lunch, and enjoy it. Look! See! They used #LovingLife hashtag, and literally, everything they own matches in a crisp neutral palette.

It's all too easy to get caught up in one of the many staged veneers that constantly surround us. There are a lot of terms that are tossed around to describe it: Photoshop Culture, the Authenticity Gap, Image Crafting, and the Highlight Reel, to name a few. They all mean the same thing. They're all smoke and mirrors. A façade. Full of shit.

No one is required to air their dirty laundry or share their struggles in a public or visible way. We're all entitled to our privacy and are not under any requirement to show audiences any aspect of our lives. Social Media has blurred the lines on privacy, but I am here to remind you, you are still allowed to have a private life.

However —

(a big, however)

— there are moral and ethical implications, and even legal limitations, from being outright deceitful when it comes to selling a good or service. False advertising laws may not include language specifically on creating phony or exaggerated digital lifestyle personas, but it sure as shit isn't okay to pretend to be someone you're not or have a lifestyle you don't in order to bilk people out of their money. It makes you an asshole and a con artist.

Combine this with predatory marketing and advertising, and add on a sprinkle of the psychological impact that social media has on our well-being; it is a recipe for some straight-up, solid gold manipulation.

The highlight reels.

There are several factors at play here that make our brains vulnerable to the impact of social media and digital advertising. Breaking the fourth wall for a moment, Michelle is a marketing executive specializing in digital marketing and social media. This is her day in and day out.

Let's start by acknowledging the magnitude of our daily exposure to advertising. First, we are exposed to anywhere from 6,000 to 10,000 ads each day, with each one of them encouraging us to spend, spend, spend (Carr, 2023). That, right there, is extraordinarily strong and consistent messaging encouraging us to be in a consumer mindset constantly.

Yeah. That's right. Thousands. Do you think that's a crazy number? Try this one on for size: the average person makes 35,000 decisions per day (Graff, 2022).

Every time I tell someone this statistic (yes, I've really used this stat in regular conversation more than once), they're always shocked that it's so high, and they don't recall doing *that much*.

That's because we don't consciously make 95% of our decisions. The sub- and unconscious minds do most of it for us (Morse, 2014).

Meaning we often cannot articulate on a surface level why we make the choices we make. This is our autopilot mode; these are fast and automatic decisions, relying heavily on cognitive biases and meaning by association.

This lack of active reasoning leaves our brains susceptible to the manipulative and potentially misleading effects of our ingrained biases and our environment — like our tendency as humans to seek out information that confirms existing beliefs and ignore or dismiss information that contradicts them. Hence the polarized society we live in now.

This is just one of many biases that affect our ability to think critically, and how to exploit these biases is something skilled marketers have long known.

I am going to skip the lengthy list of biases our brains make when we're making decisions. I want to keep my promise of being brief, but the takeaway from this is that our brain is very susceptible to a variety of different biases, which strongly influence how we process information and respond to the world around us, often in an involuntary capacity.

Here is one more good example to keep in your back pocket, though:

Color.

Research shows that most people make subconscious judgments within 0.05 seconds of seeing something, whether it is a person or a product (Laja, 2022); 90% of these subconscious judgments are based on color alone (Patel, 2020). Our previously held associations with different colors, such as associating white with cleanliness or pink with femininity, directly impact the decisions we make every day. Which also explains why nearly everything I own is black or green.

The number of ads we see each day has increased exponentially since the dawn of the Information Era. The internet, social media, and smartphones are a consumer-driven economy's best friend. You are completely reachable all the time and glued to digital platforms that are actively monitoring your activity with those annoying cookie popups and tactics like cross-application tracking. Companies even use your GPS coordinates to gather data on your location/movements and habits.

This data is funneled into complex algorithms that pop out near-perfect access to very targeted audiences that companies pay handsomely to use. We see it everywhere: suggestions on that new must-have item to purchase based on our search history or a new account to follow based on our other interactions. The platforms want to keep your gaze on their site as much as possible, so they push content tailored to you to keep you there. We're so accustomed to these personalized experiences, and they do come in handy, but we should also see that this is a cautionary tale. These are prolific techniques to influence our decision-making *that work.*

I'm not suggesting in the slightest that all marketing and advertising is immoral or anything of the sort. What I am trying to express is that we need to be mindful of the effects of marketing on our decision-making and to take a critical eye on some of the conclusions we draw about a person, product, or company. We are seeing very selective sharing or editing of content to present a more desirable or idealized image that is often far from reality.

Dopamine is a hell of a drug.

Ah, dopamine, the brain's neurotransmitter extraordinaire. The Oz of our mind, a messenger pulling the strings on the reward and pleasure centers of our brain. Also, the force behind our motivation, learning, and reinforcement. Basically, the good stuff.

Common activities and experiences that can give our dopamine levels a boost include such wicked delights like things covered in cheese and other high fat/sugar content food; exercising and adrenaline pumping activities; listening to music and engaging in creative pursuits; as well as going on spending sprees, learning something new, finishing tasks or achievements, and feeling validated (McLean Hospital, 2023).

As social media platforms often have features such as likes, comments, and follower counts, when users are at the receiving end of a new follower or likes on a post, it also leads to a release of dopamine in our brain, making us feel all warm and tingly (McLean Hospital, 2023). Each like and comment validates us and reinforces the messaging that if I do x action, I will be rewarded with a rush of dopamine.

The constant stream of new and potentially exciting content also triggers a dopamine release, even with just the *anticipation* of discovering something interesting or novel while we endlessly scroll. It's instant, and our brains like instant gratification — putting us into a cycle of anticipation and reward that is *addicting*. You know, like drugs (McLean Hospital, 2023).

Similarly, but often more intensely, drugs hijack our dopamine system, lighting up the brain's reward circuitry and causing a surge of dopamine to flood our minds. That's why people do drugs. It feels good. That's why people post selfies of a filtered, idealized life. That is why people scroll social media. That's why people get runner's highs and love eating pizza. It feels good.

And it feels good because our friend, dopamine, is creating intense feelings of euphoria. At the same time, the dopamine flood psychologically reinforces our desire to repeat the drug-taking behavior, even if your drug of choice is Instagram — or cheese sticks.

Dopamine is essential to our brain chemistry, and adequate levels are necessary to live a healthy life. Remember, while these activities can give us a dopamine boost, and there is nothing wrong with that, it's important to seek a healthy balance and avoid excessive or addictive behaviors.

Exercise: *Reflect on any dopamine-inducing behaviors you typically complete in a day. Or spend a day actively considering what's happening around you when you notice the rush.*

Write it down and describe the sensations around each activity and consider what it was about each event that caused the rush of "feel good" neurotransmitters.

Do you notice any patterns? Do you feel like any are getting to be "too much"?

Chapter 3:

We all gotta cope somehow.

"Coping is about embracing the storms of life and learning to dance in the rain."

— Unknown

Look, life is an absolute shit show. We're all just trying our best to keep our heads above water. I am not shitting on or judging anyone for the dopamine-inducing activities you use to keep sane and keep going, AKA your coping mechanisms. Coping mechanisms exist for a reason; they help us through tough or stressful times. A crutch that we may need just simply to survive this moment. And that is o-fucking-kay.

Note: I'm not referring to an addiction that interrupts your ability to function in your daily life and your relationships. A coping mechanism is very different from an addiction; addictions typically require professional intervention.

But if you're here reading this book, it's a pretty safe bet that you're looking to make changes and live a better life. Part of living a better life is cutting out some of the less healthy habits we form or switching to different coping mechanisms.

In this chapter, we'll go over how to make some healthy changes, but as we all know, change isn't easy. Lasting change is even harder. I have been trying to kick my junk food habit for literal decades. Have you tried junk food? It's delicious.

Almond butter is not the same as peanut butter. Kale chips are not nearly as tasty or crunchy as potato chips. Fries are just a flat-out better experience than eating baked zucchini sticks.

These are just facts. But another fact is that junk food also hurts your health, whereas kale most definitely does not.

While I still dollop in the fine art of snacking on the likes of a box of buttery Ritz Crackers because it's been a fucking day, I have made significant changes to my daily life that look more like the kale chips side of decision-making.

I've cut soda completely from my diet after a very long love affair with Diet Coke and exchanged it instead for lemon water. I drink banana smoothies with spinach every morning instead of having no breakfast and a sugary latte. I made real changes that have positively impacted my health and have directly led me to achieve my goal of living a healthier life.

Change takes time. It also takes some grit, perseverance, and self-compassion along the way. Below are a few ways to make it a little easier for yourself to make change happen.

Time triage and check marks.

Again, I want to highlight once more that forming new habits to reach your goals, be it in your personal life, your health, your career ambitions, starting a business, or whatever, are just that: they're new. They're not "good," and the current habits you want to amend are not "bad." They just are.

Labeling things "good" or "bad" just causes a shame spiral. Don't beat yourself up. Please. The habits you have formed may not be ideal for your goals at this juncture, but they were often created either as a learned experience as a child (so very deeply ingrained) or they came about as a way to keep you going. They served you to get you to this point, and there is real value in that. But now, they may no longer serve your best interests, and you're ready to move on.

This mindset is crucial because it reflects self-care and self-compassion, two things that are absolutely vital to making any lasting changes and finding happiness. The more you shame yourself for doing x, or being y, or not doing z, the harder you are making it for yourself to move on. Shame just leads to repeating the same behaviors and feeding into feelings of negative self-worth. And when you feel shitty about yourself, it's kind of hard to maintain motivation, right?

Another thing to keep in mind when taking more active steps to change, learn something new, and create new habits, is that speed doesn't matter at fucking all. What matters is the consistency you put in to move toward your goals.

I mean, I get it; we live in an era of instant gratification and literally instant everything. Smartphones, the Internet of Things, Amazon Prime, 5G, Netflix, emails, etc., etc. etc., are these incredible tech advances that have made our lives easier. They have also facilitated the speed and instant demand we have for info, answers, movies, communication, and Christmas gift shopping. It all just arrives in a fraction of the time it used to take.

Back in the day, people would use mail-order catalogs to buy clothes and gifts. They would send their order requests by snail mail and wait for their selections to be delivered by mail. That shit took weeks. Not same-day delivery with the press of a button on your magic rectangle.

These are incredible advancements in technology and ones that I use every day. But like anything else in this world, there's always a drawback. That drawback is our shortened attention spans and patience for results. Never an easy thing to wait, and we've collectively made it even harder. Now, our own patience with things such as personal growth and development, losing weight, learning a new language, mastering a new skill, etc., are also reflecting this pressure to see instant results. This isn't abnormal…but it's also not great. These are things that just take time, and we must exercise patience to persevere and create meaningful change.

In response to waning levels of patience, remind yourself that when you're working towards your goals, maybe starting your own business, learning how to code, or building up your confidence, it takes work, time, and dedication. There is literally nothing, absolutely nothing, that will be able to replace those three things.

Yeah, you can find temporary shortcuts for sure, but I'm talking about lasting change. No fad diets, no cleanses that literally just give you diarrhea and dehydration for a week, and no miracle online courses, algorithms, services, or products can replace it. And like I said in previous chapters, anyone selling you on "overnight success" is full of shit. They either don't have success and are lying, or they endured a ton of struggle until they reached their desired levels of success, and you just didn't see the hard parts.

Do not fret. Friendly reminder that I have some practical tips that I've learned in my blank number of years alive. These will help you stay the course, keep motivated and accomplish what you've started. You deserve to see it through.

First, the best way to achieve anything is to make time for it, so start time triaging.

There will never be enough hours in the day. And if you're waiting for the stars to magically align before you start writing that book (self-referential!), switch your career, or learn how to speak Spanish to spend a summer in South America, whatever it is, the stars will not align on their own. Time will not magically appear. It will never be completely perfect and fall into place.

YOU HAVE TO MAKE THE FUCKING TIME.

Yeah, it's a bummer. Once upon a time (honestly, not that long ago), I was one of the-stars-must-align kind of person — just waiting for the "right time." Fun fact, there's no such thing.

If you want something, you need to start actively scheduling it into your life at regular intervals. It doesn't

have to be all or nothing. It can be as simple as 5 minutes a day before work or a half hour every Saturday morning. Whatever. It's your schedule.

Start small and allow yourself small increments to get used to this new installment in your life. Plus, bite-sized commitments also prevent feeling overwhelmed, which often results in bailing before you really get into it.

If you try to run a marathon when first starting to long-distance run, and you're gauging your success by how close you are to completing the full 26.2 miles, you are not going to be a happy camper with a one-mile performance. Of course, you're going to feel like your efforts are futile like you can't do it, when you still have 25 miles to go, and you're exhausted at Mile 1. You're setting yourself up for failure. Finishing the marathon is the end part, not your beginning.

A more reasonable increment would be running for 10 - 15 minutes 3 times a week and seeing how that feels. It's you against you. Are you better than you were last week? Last month? Last year? That is change; that is progress.

Who cares if your friend can run marathons in her sleep? She started off 10 minutes at a time, at one point, too. But you need to remember that last week you could only run for five minutes, and now you are up to 10. You should care and celebrate that you have progressed towards your goal and you have doubled your time. Literally, nobody else matters in this situation — just you.

With time triaging, begin by evaluating how you are spending your days. Are there things that are "time wasters" you can cut back on to insert time for a new habit? Can you skip the morning social media scroll and instead spend 15 minutes on something new? You can still scroll after, don't just remove things entirely or right away; this isn't all or nothing. You're just making space for something new, not playing an all-or-nothing game.

This also means learning how to prioritize and accept a little more imperfection. We would all love to have daily bougie meals worthy of an Instagram pic, houses that are always spotless, and laundry that is always folded and put away. But we're not Oprah (unless Oprah is reading this, then please give me a call) with private chefs and household staff making this all possible.

However, if you can afford to outsource some life requirements to free up time, then awesome, do that. Hire some help with cleaning, meals, childcare, etc. For example, I get my groceries delivered. I fucking hate the chaotic nature of grocery stores and the dystopian realism involved in attempts to scoop up a non-wilted cilantro bunch without it ending in some knockoff version of *The Hunger Games*. Delivery costs a bit extra, and it's always a gamble with what I end up receiving and the quality of my cilantro, but it frees up my time and emotional bandwidth quite dramatically so I can focus on my priorities. I have accepted that less-than-perfect groceries and a little more cash are a fair trade-off for more time.

I also know I am not going to fold and hang up all my laundry, so I bought bins, and I shove pretty much all my clothes into said bins without any real sense of organization. But my laundry is put away, and I don't constantly see a laundry basket full of clothes, making me feel guilty with every glance for not dealing with it yet.

The bins mean I can skip the laundry eating away at my emotional energy. The result is I have clean clothes, I'm able to keep up with my laundry, and yeah, maybe deal with a few more wrinkles and restricting my ability to visualize my wardrobe. But, as I mentioned, I also get to avoid the guilt and shame that pop up every time I used to see those full hampers and laundry baskets harshly judging me as I walk by. Fuckers.

Time management is one of the best tools you can utilize to make sustainable lifestyle changes. Things like my bin example may free up your time dramatically, and there are plenty of apps to help you gain even more control of your schedule. There are an astonishing number of apps, free or paid, such as the likes of Monday.com, Clockify, Asana, Jira, and Slack, to help you. Just start looking and reviewing what's out there and consider if you're willing to spend money on it or look for free versions.

I recommend testing out several to see what works best. There is no "right" solution. It just depends on what works for you and what you're hoping to get out of it. It's like dating; you don't have to marry the first person to buy you dinner.

Some common points to consider:

Do you need an analysis of how you're spending your time? Some apps will help you calculate where the most abundant "time wasters" are and recommend strategies. This may also help pinpoint where you can offload certain tasks based on how much time you're spending vs. the cost to hire out. Perhaps you need reminders to keep a routine and like seeing the progress recorded. Or maybe something more social to help keep you motivated? Research what's around and consider what approaches could help you better understand and manage your time, then look to see if there's an app for that. There usually is.

Using an app to help manage your time is not your only option. I prefer to go analog. I make use of agendas and calendars to organize upcoming deadlines, important events, and my top priorities. The act of physically writing tasks down on paper helps to clarify my thoughts. I feel like I need to get everything out somewhere I can see it, then from there, I typically start organizing my thoughts and my tasks and evaluating my priorities. Do I really need to finish the cover design this week, or am I just overwhelming my schedule? Do I have to finish cleaning the house today, or can I split it up over three days to make it feel less cumbersome/energy-draining?

Plus, physically crossing off things on your to-do list IS A RUSH, Y'ALL. Even if there is only one thing on the priority list you want to ensure gets done, completing it and then crossing that task off your list generates a great sense of satisfaction — the dopamine hit. Seriously, try it out for one day and see how you feel.

The task list completions should also include items that require asking for help and/or outsourcing. You don't have to be the one doing it; it just needs to get done. You get credit for those, too.

Another effective tool is to cut down on "time wasters" like your social media consumption by setting a timer. You can still enjoy these activities, whether it's video games, TikTok, watching TV, or staring at a blank wall — the timer creates structure and accountability that will aid in prioritizing your time. Don't get me wrong, spending time on activities that help us disengage, unwind, or relax and have value. You can and should still enjoy these activities without feeling guilty or consumed by them. For example, if you pull out your phone first thing to scroll each morning, strike a better balance by setting a 15-minute timer. When it goes off, put your phone down and take care of your business. Feed your dog, make a healthy breakfast, or go for a short walk.

Only you will know what will best fit your needs, and it is totally valid to want to continue enjoying TV or your daily social media scroll. But just like junk food, moderation is key. Eat those Doritos. Watch Succession (seriously, watch Succession, it's so good), but there's a plethora of research and wide acknowledgment that too much-processed food and too much screen time are not beneficial for your health. These things still have their place in your life, so let them be in it, but in moderation.

With that, please also consider how you approach the flipside. As in, when implementing a new habit or change, it doesn't need to feel like pure torture or like you are devoid of all the joy you used to have in your life. Instead, you can make it easier on yourself by creating positive associations. If you're trying just to limit screen time but don't know what else to do with that time, instead, try something new you've been curious about, like a book, puzzle, podcast, or just enjoying looking outside. The time off from the screen should not feel like a chore, or the habit will be even harder to break because instead of getting the dopamine rush from the likes of social media, you've replaced it with something that sucks, and now you're filled with dread.

I've always found it easier to listen to music or an audiobook or podcast when doing something unpleasant like washing the dishes or going to the gym. Not only does it help distract me from the fact that I am not overly comfortable or having the time of my life — such as when I first started working out and felt very self-conscious. It also makes the time pass more quickly. I typically bring my iPad or iPhone to watch something funny while on the bike or elliptical, and while I know that watching the show in bed eating snacks would be more my speed, my association with gym time is now related to the laughter and enjoyment I get from watching an episode of whatever I have earmarked for that activity. My dread lessens with each repeat, and yours will, too.

Learning to take more control of your time will be a huge factor in your ability to inspire change and achieve your goals.

Exercise: *Make a list of what you currently prioritize in your life, then make a separate list and list what you want your top priorities to be, such as family, health, career, hobbies, etc. Then, evaluate if there are differences between the two lists.*

Consider how much time you currently devote to each priority.

Reflect on whether your time allocation aligns with your values and consider adjustments to ensure a better balance.

Chapter 4:

Slow your roll and get some

goals.

"Authenticity is a collection of choices that we have to make every day. It's about the choice to show up and be real. The choice, to be honest. The choice to let our true selves be seen."

– Dr. Brene Brown

It is not weird or abnormal, and there is nothing wrong with you if you don't know what your goals are or if you haven't set any yet. You will by the end of this book.

Doing something like this requires you to slow down, set time aside to reflect, research, take notes, think, watch YouTube videos, and ponder more. In this modern era, we often prioritize "getting things done" and neglect the crucial aspect of putting ourselves first. We are a results-oriented society, and it is literally killing us. Seriously, look it up.

As a whole, we are a generation of people struggling to make it through each day. We are in a mental health crisis. We are financially strapped, overworked, underpaid, and living in a time where disconnecting from work feels impossible. Companies continue to downsize but increase workloads (Seppälä, 2017). We are also the most productive we've ever been but at the cost of our health. (Growing Inequalities, n.d.)

I know, I know. Slowing down and putting in time to connect with yourself and your desires sounds insane. I have been that person when I read or hear someone say something like, "You need to take time to get to know yourself" or "Take time for self-care." Time? Like, are you fucking kidding me?

Unless "getting to know me" can be shoehorned somewhere between making dinner, grocery shopping, doing laundry, picking up the kids, taking the kids to sports, answering emails, working over eight hours a day, etc., you can go fuck a bag of glass. There is no way I can manage adding on another task not essential to surviving the minimum requirements of being an adult. Also, I prefer to sleep at some point rather than trying some hippie-dippie, meditate with a crystal, and reflect on my life's purpose shit, you absolute, new-age nut job. It must be nice to have that time.

Yeah, it is nice to have that time, by the way. But I had to fight for it, and it was not easy.

Whoever you are, single or married, with or without kids, being overwhelmed and neglecting yourself is an all too real experience for many of us in the modern world. Numerous studies and research conducted in the recent past have illuminated that even in a double-income household, women are more than shouldering the brunt of housework and childcare compared to men. And for those of you stepping up to be an equal partner — cool, but I'm not going to throw you a parade for doing shit women have been thanklessly doing for decades without an ounce of credit. For the rest of you, get your shit together and start helping without being asked.

Anyway —

It is impossible to do everything and have enough time for yourself. We've covered this in previous chapters. But what we didn't talk about is that setting time aside for things without tangible outcomes, like starting a new business, courses, etc., tends to be viewed as superfluous. A frivolous activity. I cannot begin to stress enough that to really change your life and everything around it, the center of all this needs to be you. Understanding what you want, what your limitations are, what your priorities are, what you don't want, what your fears are, your strengths, your insecurities, all of it.

Because once you know who you are and what you want, everything else will start to fall into place. Living in self-alignment means the actions we take reflect our beliefs and values, reducing the weight and impact of internal conflicts. It allows us to live an authentic life, increasing feelings of self-worth and overall satisfaction in the decisions we make.

When you are right with yourself, the best version of you will show up in every other part of your own life. This better version of yourself will show up for others, too, and dramatically improve your relationships, your quality of life, and your performance on and off the job, and allow you to be genuinely happier.

But…it doesn't come without sacrifice.

Just like I mentioned in the previous chapter, this is another habit or task that requires a little lifestyle change. It doesn't need to be drastic, like trying to fit in a Zumba class three times a week. It literally can be five minutes every day before the world awakens and starts screaming its demands at you. It can be in the bathroom stall at work for five minutes in between meetings. It can be in the parked car before you start driving to pick someone up or on your commute. That's it — just five minutes for you to take that first step.

In those five minutes, it's time to start getting to know what's important to you and what you want from life. Do a five-minute meditation. Start a Pinterest board of what you'd like life to look like, write it down in a notebook you carry, or type it up somewhere safe on your phone. Scribble on the back of a receipt. Or even just keep a Rolodex (dated reference!) in your head if it seems too overwhelming to write it down at first. That's okay. You do this at your pace and in whatever way feels right to you.

The idea is not to feel overwhelmed and to give yourself permission to take whatever break in whatever way you need to without it being burdensome. Over time, I guarantee that these couple-minute emotional vacations will begin to change your mood and will start expanding their impact on other mindful practices and efforts of self-care. But we start where we can.

Remember, it's you vs. you. Not what the influencer said or your friend did. It's what works for you and you only.

Once you start gaining a clearer picture of what you want out of life, it's time to start setting goals. I cannot stress enough the importance of writing these down and working through the equations of what it takes to make them happen — breaking them up into reasonable baby steps along the way and acknowledging every tiny bit of progress.

There are a million resources online and free worksheets, podcasts, TED talks, etc., on the mechanics of goal setting. In one of your 5-minute timeouts, take a look at what's out there and what seems like it could work for you. There is no one way to approach it, and it may take more than one shot. This is not a one-size-fits-all solution. Your life is more complicated than a beach towel; you may need to check out a few different dimensions.

Going forward, I encourage you to create five short-term goals and at least one long term. Think of short-term goals that may take a week or two to accomplish. These will most certainly aid in keeping you motivated for the longer ones. We all need a win every now and then to keep going.

Short-term goals can be as simple as donating to Goodwill and finally getting rid of those jeans from six years ago that you are not going to wear again. Don't forget to get the receipt. It's a tax write-off (wink). Or going on four ten-minute walks in one week. Just make it about you and something you know will better your life just a little. As you finish one, cross it off and immediately replace it with another.

In turn, this will build momentum and make it easier to continue chipping away bit by bit on the big one. That earned sense of accomplishment is significant in being able to stay the course.

An example of a long-term goal could be something such as finishing school, saving for a car, or getting your own/new place. You get the idea. It just needs to be something that will take you more than a few weeks to achieve.

Be sure to allow yourself to recognize progress, even when you're not at the end goal. Running a 10K is an incredible feat; it doesn't need to be the whole marathon to allow yourself to feel proud and recognize your progress. It's the learned ability to see progress in baby steps that will allow you to stay the course, and you deserve every ounce of that recognition.

When you pick a significant goal to accomplish, such as running that marathon when you have not run in years or setting a goal to save $10,000 for a down payment on a new home, with a savings account balance capable of rolling its eyes as you; it's a normal reaction to feel like a gladiator who just stepped into the battlefield with a wooden spoon as a weapon. Again, this is a totally normal reaction.

Big goals should scare you, and we're going to talk about that next.

Bravery feels fucking awful.

"Courage doesn't always roar. Sometimes courage is the quiet voice at the end of the day that says, 'I will try again tomorrow.'"

– Mary Anne Radmacher

I'm going to let you in on a secret I didn't learn until later in life. It has since changed my life and my approach to everything. Setting goals that are important to you takes vulnerability. It means admitting what is important to you, getting out of your comfort zone, telling the world what you want and who you are, and accepting that if it doesn't work out, it is going to hurt. Really hurt. It requires bravery — a lot of it. And being brave NEVER feels good. See above.

Seriously. It feels great after the fact; you feel like you can take on Godzilla with a flamethrower and tell your boss to eat a bag of dicks. This well-earned surge of dopamine and confidence comes after you've done the hard part of finding the grit and inner strength to step up and take action. But that's not the brave part. That's the reward.

I know for me, growing up (and even now), the brave hero stories we hear/see in movies, books, TV, etc., are usually of the warrior, fearless in the eyes of danger, overcoming risky situations and villains without so much of a blink of an eye.

That's not bravery.

Bravery can **only** exist when despite the fear you feel, you give it your all.

It is not dependent on whether you pull it off, have a flawless execution, or even finish the job. **Bravery is when you show up in the face of your fears, doubts, insecurities, and anxieties — and you try anyway.**

It will be messy. It will not be a flawless performance. It will not be without mistakes. It will not be a smooth, easy ride or look like a montage in a movie. You probably won't look cool doing it. I never do. I always look more like an awkward and uncoordinated pelican. However, you can wear a cape or a leather outfit if you want to look more hero-esque, but it's not required. You do you, boo.

Bravery is in those moments when you feel your conviction waver, you feel like throwing in the towel, or you feel like you've bitten off more than you can chew. Or you've dropped all your groceries and ugly cried for ten minutes solid in the stairwell leading up to your apartment door, rambling off about how you just can't take it anymore.

Know that the wavering conviction or the stairway meltdown has nothing to do with the groceries and everything to do with the bigger battle you're fighting — it's in those moments where you let yourself feel and acknowledge the struggle, the pain, the fear, the doubt, but then slowly pick up the groceries and continue walking up the stairs. **THAT** is what bravery looks like.

When those times come — and they will —, please don't let your feelings of discouragement or your fear of failure stop you. The opposite of success is not failure; it's mediocrity. Failure is an inevitable part of success, as is bravery. You cannot cheat the system; you will have to struggle if you want to push past your self-imposed (or externally created) limitations and achieve the worthwhile. You will have to feel the discomfort and fear and overcome the mental burden that comes with it. Otherwise, you have destined yourself always to be and have less than you are capable of.

My intention is not to scare you but instead, empower you to take on the necessary mindset to push yourself past the struggles that will come. Acknowledge the struggles for what they are, and let yourself feel afraid, overwhelmed, or apprehensive. Even in the admission of struggle, we show strength and bravery in our vulnerability. There is so much power in that, and it offers a way to deeply connect with others facing the same obstacles — making us feel less alone. When we show vulnerability, we give others permission to do the same. And it makes the road forward a lot less daunting.

You are braver than you think you are.

Life may be tough, but so are you.

One step at a time, please.

So far, we've covered quite a bit on how change, the pursuit of your goals, and how bravery is not going to resemble the feeling of cuddling kittens or taking a nap in the sun on a quiet Sunday — but now we're going to look at tactics to keep on truckin'.

First, we briefly covered the importance of starting small and setting achievable milestones along the way. Depending on the goal, this could mean doing some research and discovering what it takes to get it done and learning from others who have done similar and how they approached it.

For example, if your goal is to become a lawyer, then longer-term planning and a lot of research is necessary. You'll need to take the LSAT, which means signing up for an exam date and studying for the LSAT. After that, you'll need to begin the search for a university that aligns with your goals. Make a list of your top five. Be sure you carefully research the prerequisites of each, as they can differ. Have a clear understanding of what your financing needs are like and research any necessary funding options. Consider whether you can manage attending PT while still working. Sometimes you can lighten the load during the semester by reading the required texts the summer before getting started. The list goes on, but you get the idea.

The important thing to understand here is that you do not need to have all the answers figured out for every step of the process right now. But by understanding that for the next year, the focus needs to be on the LSAT, and after that exam, you can start planning the next part of the journey. Practice your new mindset. One step at a time will get you there.

Breaking down your goal into smaller, manageable tasks will help you avoid feeling overwhelmed and allow you to focus on the most immediate steps and improve your probability of surviving the long haul.

Go get you some validation.

Another important factor in staying the course is receiving encouragement and affirmations along the way. Yes, many of us have heard the conventional wisdom that "the only opinion that matters is yours." This is true to an extent, but most of us do not live in the forest by ourselves and only need the birds and squirrels to keep us company.

Human beings, by their very nature, are social creatures. It is a widely accepted and proven fact that within our hierarchy of basic needs, human connection is a key component of turning out adults capable of functioning within a modern society.

When we connect with other people, especially the important ones in our lives that we love and value, their opinion is going to matter to us. And it is a normal human need to seek validation and affirmation beyond yourself. Perhaps the most enlightened Buddhist monk does not, but they are the exception and not the rule.

For the rest of us, we will always be working through the balancing act of navigating our ability to self-affirm and seek reinforcement and feedback from the outside world. There is no golden ratio, and it will constantly fluctuate throughout your life. But it's okay to need someone to tell you that you're doing great, they're proud of you, or that you got this (and you do). And you look nice today.

Outside of seeking words of encouragement from our social circle, one of the most effective ways to boost your motivation is by exposing yourself to motivational talks. This can be a powerful tool in finding inspiration and motivation to allow yourself even to dream big and will carry on motivating you when you take the first, fifth, 87th, or 304th step.

Seriously, it works. There is literal neurological science and psychology backing this up. Motivational talks are more than purveyors of hope and inspiration; they activate our brain's reward pathways. Once again, dopamine shows up for a good time.

Typically, inspiring or motivational talks/speeches involve a speaker sharing their well-crafted stories and using positive language. This will naturally activate the release of dopamine, the neurotransmitter responsible for our feelings of pleasure and motivation, and will often trigger other feel-good neurotransmitters like serotonin and adrenaline as well. This will reinforce our sense of reward and evoke positive emotions with the topic.

These inspiring talks also stimulate neuroplasticity, our brain's ability to effortlessly rewire itself, as well as form new neural connections. As motivational speakers typically introduce new ideas or perspectives, our brain's way of adapting to new information and concepts is to reorganize and form new connections. This enables us to develop new habits, skills, and beliefs because it is physically — and very literally — changing the way we think (MSEd, 2022).

There's a lot more physical and mental impact than what I've just covered, but I think you get this idea. I just want to highlight one more benefit. When we listen to TED talks, go to a motivational seminar, find a YouTube channel of motivational speeches, or even just witness someone perform an action, our brains react the same way as if we were the ones performing the action. We experience a sort of mental simulation where we feel what the other person feels. This is called neural mirroring and creates a profound sense of connection, empathy, and relatability — making us more likely to identify with a speaker's experience and feel like we share in this motivation and sense of accomplishment (Acharya & Shukla, 2012).

So, if you're in need of a temporary boost or some conveniently packaged advice, motivational speakers are here to remind you that sometimes in life, we can just borrow that cup of sugar, that sprinkle of enthusiasm, and that dash of inspiration from the likes of Brene Brown, Oprah Winfrey, or whoever resonates with you.

What's also interesting is that you may not even realize this at the time, but by making progress toward your goal, you can inspire others around you to reevaluate their own dreams and aspirations. Imagine, because of your unwavering commitment to walk or run every day, someone close to you with poor health, who was struggling with unhealthy lifestyle choices, is now also walking daily. You have become a source of inspiration and motivation for them, just as others were for you.

Accountability robots.

For like 99% of the people out there, we need someone or something to hold us accountable. This is where virtual tools can come in handy. You can use them to help manage your money, set step goals for daily walking, learn a new language, or start your business. The possibilities are endless because there's almost always an app or smart product already out there meant to keep you going.

One of the most accessible types of virtual assistance you can find is in the health and fitness arena. If you are using a fitness or health app, you can easily set reasonable goals using the suggestions an app provides. Do a little research, check the ratings, and then pick an app that fits you best.

One of the things I love most about a good health and fitness app is the ability to join virtual groups or form your own teams where you share your goals each week or compete against one another. A team dynamic or friendly competition provides a boost of accountability for your actions and efforts, as well as helps maintain longer-term commitments. Healthy bodies are more than just steps walked each day, time spent exercising, or diet-related, and many of these apps include a wide variety of healthy habit-building challenges such as drinking water, sleeping goals, meditation, etc. Examples of collaborative apps include MyFitnessPal, Stride, and Challenge Accepted.

Regardless of your goal, these types of apps typically exist for virtually every aspect of our lives. If that's not your style, you can go old school and print out calendars and worksheets to stay accountable and measure progress.

Whatever it is, take time to invest in researching and setting up a system that will help you stay the course and keep organized because you and your goals are worth that effort.

When you're feeling tapped out.

When you first set a significant goal, you might find it relatively easy to diligently apply yourself to the work involved because you and your motivation are flying high.

<Enters life to fuck shit up.>

Sooner or later, however, you will have an off day, hit a roadblock, or encounter some bullshit that just steamrolls you or knocks you off course.

Because life and shit happen.

If you expect an elongated, serene stretch of time where everything effortlessly falls into place, allowing you to maintain unwavering focus and a constant state of exhilaration to complete all your tasks, then the reality is going to bitch slap you across the face.

Whether it's your career, kids, personal life, romantic relationships, your pets, or your NFT collection of lizards in jaunty hats, there will always be ebbs and flows of the good, the bad, the ugly, and the wtf.

These less-than-ideal life events can kick your ass, then kick you some more when you're already down, and then throw salt and lemon juice on the wounds. You may feel demotivated, discouraged, and apathetic, making it harder to get through the day, let alone even harder for you to reach your goals.

And it's okay to feel these things. It's okay to have doubts. That isn't a sign that you can't do this or you're not the kind of person that is "meant to do it" Every single one of those people we admire that have accomplished incredible feats, didn't just wake up every day psyched to get their ass kicked and feed off hearing "no." If they say that, they're fucking lying.

But it's when you're in these lows to take care of yourself, practice self-compassion, and make a conscious decision to get past it and keep going. This doesn't mean just digging in deeper and spending more hours grinding away, hoping for that spark to come back. That may work for some people or at some junctures, but sometimes it also makes things much worse.

It's okay to take a break. It's okay to walk away and clear your head.

Often there are some quick fixes that can help an unfocused mind reengage, such as listening to music that gets you in the right mindset to feel amped up, inspired, creative, and energized.

Another way to refresh your mind and spirit is to go for a short walk. Fresh air and sunshine have been proven time and time again to help people feel more positive and motivated (Cheevers, 2021). Plus, the act of engaging in relaxing activities like walking allows your mind to take a necessary reset. Charles Darwin was known to take many leisurely strolls every day as part of his daily work because he knew he needed the mental space clear his mind and allow fresh reflection (On The Link Between Great Thinking and Obsessive Walking, 2021).

This is also commonly known as "shower thoughts." Ever notice that you always remember something crucial in the shower or have a genius idea or the answer you've been looking for? When I was in college, there were periods when I was taking five showers a day to find those "Aha!" moments I needed to finish a project or paper.

Distractions that interrupt your daily routine or hinder your focus present another common obstacle in maintaining motivation. This can be especially difficult during holidays or vacations when you have extra people around and/or your routine is thrown completely off-kilter. Additionally, the constant pull of social media, especially during holidays/vacations when you have interesting things to share and more free time, can also prove to be a major distraction and cause you to lose focus.

It's not uncommon to fall back into old habits even after making significant breaks from them. Don't beat yourself up when you find yourself in this situation again. With constant distractions and the revolving door of new and instantaneous demands in today's world, it's easy to get caught up and rely on old patterns to navigate new stressors or cope with rising demands. Just take a step back, reassess, and adjust where necessary. Implementing new behaviors takes time and practice. Allow yourself that grace.

If you're still having trouble, try removing whatever distractions you can from around you. I know for me, I cannot focus on anything if I'm surrounded by clutter, and I always need to simplify my work and living areas before I feel like I can do anything else. I even make my bed every day, not out of obligation or some nagging voice in my head. I do it because it makes me feel instantly more relaxed in my home to see a clean and organized space.

If the environment you're working in is a bustling part of your home and can't be changed, try letting those around you know that you're working on something important to you. You might have to limit your request for peace and no interruptions to just an hour per day (or even less), but if you keep at it each day, you will see the necessary progress.

I know this is difficult if you have children or really any aged human living with you. There seems to be some sort of magnetic pull of "important" interruptions that surface only when quiet time is requested. So, GTFO. Take your notebook, laptop, Etch-a-Sketch, stone tablet, or whatever, and sit outside or in your car. Mosey on over to a nearby park or a corner coffee shop to focus. Whatever you need to do to stay committed, even spending a couple of bucks on foam earplugs, keep in mind that some progress is always better than none — be willing to work with what you've got.

We've discussed how motivation and distractions can impact your progress toward reaching your goals and hinder your ability to maintain forward momentum. Still, possibly one of the most insidious obstacles you'll encounter will be a lack of confidence in yourself.

There is no easy fix for confidence building, but the tiniest improvement will snowball quickly into more and more progress until it unexpectedly shows up in other areas of your life. Meaning when you have a confidence boost in one area, physical health, for example, that will also boost how confident you're feeling about tackling other goals like your budget. Confidence is infectious — the good kind of infectious, not like chlamydia or something.

Now, when I feel my confidence dwindling, I get proactive. I often meditate and journal to see what's going on below the surface and causing this dip. I speak with my therapist, chat with my support network, and seek out resources or new strategies for boosting my confidence with online videos/articles, books, or even a pep talk from a friend. These help me avoid going into a negative spiral of self-defeat and help kickstart that upswing.

Many times, when I'm avoiding a difficult task, it's due to my own fears and lack of confidence that I can do it. I also have an avoidant personality type when I just flat out just don't feel like dealing with something, like my bathroom sink that is currently clogged and hasn't magically fixed itself while I have ignored its existence for a couple of days.

One trick I learned is just to dip my toe in and do the tiniest amount of work possible on that task. I use this in other parts of my life, too, like if I'm also avoiding dishes. Tell yourself that you only need to do the smallest possible amount, and that's it. You are done right after the small toe dip, no judgement. Whether it's washing one dish, writing for 10 minutes without an agenda or expectation, or running for 1 minute instead of 1 mile, do it.

Often, just that small task getting finished is enough to feed me the sense of accomplishment I need to tackle another few dishes or try running for another minute. That usually leads to another few dishes, another minute, and often the whole sink and the whole mile are complete.

Finding a way to work on that big task or etch away at a lofty goal, even for the shortest amount of time, will give you a sense of satisfaction and accomplishment that amplifies exponentially and gives your self-confidence a needed boost.

But sometimes, it won't work. And that's okay. That's a strong indicator that you need a bigger break or that there is something else that needs your attention first. You may be facing health issues, a job loss, the death of a pet or loved one, etc. All of these can knock us down and leave us feeling devastated, robbing us of our momentum.

It's important to remember that you cannot pour from an empty cup. Setting aside time for rest and relaxation is also a key component of being able to make it for the long haul. Just like a long road trip, you're going to need to stop for fuel, snacks, and bathroom breaks. But usually, after that break, you're refreshed and ready to keep going.

It is okay to hit pause. I repeat it is okay to hit pause. Do what you need to do to heal or manage your personal business, and when you're ready, get right back out there. Honor your feelings and give them the space they deserve, however long that ends up being. Once the need to honor them has passed, get back out there.

When I get tough news or have a shitty day, I usually say aloud to myself, "This sucks. And today, I'm going to be sad and cry and just feel it. But then tomorrow, I'm going to get up and try again." I do just that. I let myself cry it out, punch pillows, snap pencils, write in tear-stained notebooks and eat cookie dough with a spoon. I know I need it.

This works for me like 99% of the time. As does a shower and washing your face after a good cry. It feels like I'm wiping the slate clean after setting aside the time to feel what I need to feel.

You may or may not exude quite the same zeal after these episodes. A tough situation can throw anyone into a churning emotional thought pattern. Even after the worst is over, you may feel trapped in an emotional fog. **I often feel suffocated or confined in a cage when I can't shake off lingering pain or turmoil. It may feel like it will last forever; I know it does for me at times. But I am here to remind you that even the worst things possible will not last forever. It will pass.**

You may need to take some time off or make adjustments, but one of the best ways to recover from something hard-hitting is to focus on caring for yourself and showing yourself compassion. The cage bars often disappear the more you practice self-care like getting proper rest, eating nutritious meals, drinking enough water, being around people that help you feel connected and heard, and talking it through.

Exercise: *Consider when you have witnessed bravery in real life.*

Write down a few points about what exactly was brave about the person/situation.

Consider and jot down some points on times that you feel like you've shown bravery and why.

Chapter 5:

Unfuck yourself financially.

"Taking care of your finances is not about restriction; it's about empowering yourself to make choices that align with your goals and values."

— Unknown.

The demonstration of self-control distinguishes a child from an adult. This doesn't imply that children cannot possess self-control or that all adults have mastered their behavior. We've all encountered both the remarkably wise and composed child and the adult whose finances are a sh*tshow (hello, younger me). Nonetheless, self-control represents a certain level of maturity, even if it takes some individuals longer to attain it.

Few things will test your self-control more than learning to control your spending and manage your money wisely, especially when there's free shipping involved. Managing your money requires self-discipline and careful planning.

To control your spending and finances effectively — it is essential to track your income, monitor expenses, and develop a budgeting strategy that works for you. Going through this process will help you determine and maintain your version of a sustainable lifestyle. Protecting that lifestyle from the sting of unexpected expenses (flat tire, medical bill, hot water heater, etc.) with an emergency fund is a necessity.

Regarding goals, having money at your disposal that is not solely allocated to paying the monthly bills is crucial for helping your larger goals become a reality. Using money needed for monthly expenses on starting up your dream business is a guaranteed way to increase your anxiety and stress levels. Don't do it. Don't create a cycle of deficit.

In today's world, nothing comes without a cost. Whether it's a gift or donation, there's always a price to be paid, even if it's not immediately visible to you. It's important to remember even your time has value to truly understand this. You must first have a clear understanding of your finances and the reasons behind their current state.

For example, if you decide to reach a fitness goal by taking advantage of running outdoors because it does not cost anything compared to a gym membership, inevitably, you'll find yourself whipping out a card to pay for something. It could be anything from a good pair of running shoes, shorts, or leggings to prevent chafing thighs or even extra pairs of socks and Band-Aids due to the formation of blisters. If you keep at it, you are also likely to change your body shape in some ways, requiring you to update your wardrobe.

For some of you reading this book, money management comes easily with a basic understanding and good financial awareness. However, many struggle with it and are unsure why. This next section is designed to lay a solid foundation for better money management. If you've been battling with managing your finances or it's been a while since you actively focused on your money habits, this information can help you get back on track or inspire you to try a new approach.

Adult money habits.

Early on in my adult life, I attended an info session regarding our company's retirement benefits plan. The presenter started his schtick by asking us, "If your finances could talk, what would they say?"

I immediately blurted out, "WHAT ARE YOU DOING?" We all laughed, but we also all knew I was panicking at the thought of how financially fucked I felt.

Self-control is often seen as the epitome of maturity, but it takes more than just age to achieve it. Sometimes it's fun to buy stupid shit, no matter how old you are. However, to truly reign in our behaviors, you must recognize and confront your tendencies and limitations no matter how uncomfortable that might be. Some may shy away from self-reflection and avoid admitting they need to work on this or make funny jokes. Or avoid looking at their bank account balance. Ignorance is bliss, am I right?

Sorry, friend-o, I've got some bad news. Only by (1) accepting reality and (2) embracing and overcoming the challenges you have ahead can you truly master your own actions and become the master of your own bank account balance. You will not magically conjure a financial discipline spell and get it together without ever having to own reality. No, sadly, you must own your shit head-on like everyone else.

When handling your money, this might be an area where you've been winging it for too long. I was not raised with any guidance on how to manage my money. Because of this, I regularly overspent in my younger years, leading me not to save the money I should have. I was in debt up to my eyeballs for years. To say I was financially ill-prepared would have been an understatement. I didn't have a clue what a budget was or how to make one. I did, however, have an impressive collection of random household items with lobsters on them. You know, things that no one needs.

Before we further discuss budgets, I want you to make a new habit starting today. If you don't do this already, start logging into your bank accounts every morning and evening before you go to bed and check your balance. Review what you spent that day. You may think, *But Sara, I don't want to look... It depresses me. I prefer the land of not knowing.*

This is exactly why I'm urging you to do this. Face your spending habits. Sticking your head in the sand won't get you out of this one and onto your goal. Trust me, this one small effort makes an enormous difference in how you handle your money. **Once more, you need to own your reality before you can fix it. Be brave.**

I started my journey to improve my spending habits in that simple way. I began by checking my bank account daily with the goal of saving enough money to make a down payment on a new home. I wanted to ensure that I could afford the move, including closing costs, renting a truck, and paying for utility deposits in the new city. There are always additional costs that crop up along the way, so I added 10% to what I thought I needed as my goal.

You might think, *why not just get the deposit back from the old city and apply it to the new one for their deposit?* I'll tell you why. It takes time for it to be processed and sent to you, and this conflicted with the timing necessary to have things like the water turned on and ready for the day we needed to move in. These things cannot be done ahead of time as they require the final bill to be paid before issuing the return of the deposit, and we still needed the service at the house we were still renting until we found a suitable home. This need caused some overlap as a result and is usually a common setup as the deposits on rentals normally don't line up between move out/move in.

Prior to this, I knew I tended to overspend, and I had previously combatted this by just making sure I paid all my bills before buying any extras. However, I needed to pay more attention to my spending and rarely checked my bank account beyond making sure a purchase would not put me into overdraft, get hit with fees, or prevent me from paying another bill on time. Reaching even this level of self-control made me proud of myself. I was handling my shit. I was acting like a grown-ass adult.

My savings account, on the other hand, remained woefully empty. Occasionally, I managed to get it to a couple of hundred bucks, but I would then have to move it back to my checking account to make sure I paid all my bills on time so I could avoid late fees. So, while checking once or twice a month, when the paychecks came in helped me to not lose money; I was unable to save money for things like a down payment and emergencies.

After some painful self-reflection, I admitted to myself that I needed help. I was so tired of the money struggle. Too broke to pay for someone's help, I attended a two-day financial principles class. It was free through a local church and, to my surprise, was extremely insightful. A renowned businessman, who generously donated his time for coaching, presented it.

As time passed and I continued the habit of looking over my bank account each day, something interesting became very apparent. I was spending less. Because I was spending less, I was slowly able to accumulate more savings. This reduced so much of my day-to-day anxiety and depression that it encouraged me to go ahead and cinch in other areas of my spending where I had some control, such as my food budget. I even stopped eating out as much.

Each day I checked my account, I would see a tiny bit of progress. Within a few months, I had reached my first goal: to ensure I had saved the equivalent of one month's worth of expenses. I finally had a little safety net. Some breathing room. Never in my life had I ever been able to say this. It was such a freeing feeling. I think it was around this time that I decided I was never going back.

I bring up this experience of mine because there are a lot of stories and information out there regarding how the lack of personal finance education is a leading concern for why people struggle financially, even when their annual income is considered well above the poverty line (GoBankingRates, 2016). There are several ways this hurts a person beyond just living paycheck to paycheck and the stress and anxiety that alone causes. One of them is having no clue about the state of your checking or savings account until it is too late, which often causes additional charges and costs that deepen the void you find yourself trapped in financially.

If you're feeling overwhelmed by financial difficulties, rest assured that you're not alone. However, don't pretend the problem doesn't exist. Just as seeking medical attention for a health concern can be scary because it may confirm your worst fears, taking control of your finances can be equally daunting.

Understand that the longer you wait, the harder it will become to fix the issue. So be brave, take a look at your accounts, or your health for that matter, and tackle the problem head-on.

Whatever you need to do to make yourself face reality, do it. Take that shot of tequila. Say a quick prayer, burn sage, or do whatever, and suck it up, buttercup. It's time to acknowledge reality. Look at your accounts, the cash you have on hand, all of it. Keep track and do it every single day.

It may take weeks or months for you to see changes, but they will come as you develop more self-control and apply it to your spending habits. The faster you make changes, the faster you will progress. The more you do, the better off you will be. Believe me when I tell you that every good business owner watches their money daily as well. It is an essential financial habit for both personal and business goals alike.

Practice this newfound self-discipline and reduce your exposure to subscriber emails, social media, and platforms that constantly bombard you with irresistible ads and stories, wasting both your time and money with targeted temptations. There are other more important places where you can spend that time and money, even if that kitchen gadget looks like it'll change your meal prep game for the better.

You are not a financial wizard.

Many of us, myself included, are big proponents of "wingin' it" when it comes to a wide variety of things in our lives. But when it comes to money, that is one habit that must be broken. Leave improv to the professionals.

Financial planning is essential if you want to start a business. Investors, banks, and grant applications all require having a business and financial plan. On a personal level, to pay cash for a brand-new car without relying on a loan, you must plan ahead. If you aspire to make a down payment on your dream home, planning is imperative. Even for smaller purchases, such as a new couch or TV, understanding your finances and having a plan in place is necessary.

But before we go on, your initial step in managing your finances should be to establish an emergency fund. I call mine my "oh shit fund." Emergencies are never, oh yay, I get to save money. They always cost money and usually require a few expletives to get through.

Establishing an emergency fund is a widely recommended practice for overcoming debt and reducing stress in unexpected situations — such as a malfunctioning water heater or paying for physiotherapy after a fall. Without the necessary funds, these events can cause an already anxious and stressful situation to turn into an all-out disaster. Don't add more stress because past versions of yourself shrugged off that rainy day fund and spent it on collectible Holiday Barbies or an all-inclusive vacation. Future, you will thank yourself for not being a dipshit and spending the money frivolously — ultimately making a bad situation worse.

By having an emergency fund in place, you can handle these emergencies with peace of mind and without added financial strain.

How big should your emergency fund be? A myriad of financial institutions and debt relief programs recommend that an emergency fund consists of at least three to six months' worth of expenses. This is considered the bare minimum needed to keep a roof over your head, food in your belly, medical care, transportation for work or school, and other necessities for yourself and your family (Galvis, 2021).

Yeah, I laughed at that idea, too. This doesn't mean that you are expected to save that entire amount immediately, especially if things are tight and you are dealing with debts other than a home mortgage, car, or other obligations related to keeping that roof over your head. Most people start with an initial goal of $1,000. You have the power to set your own savings target but challenge yourself to reach it. If it can only be $500, then start there and build on it. To make this a reality, you must exercise self-control and restrict spending where you can in order to work towards building up your emergency fund as quickly as possible. Remember, something is always better than nothing.

Starting an emergency fund can be made easier by taking steps to increase your cash flow, even just for a one-time cash influx to get the ball rolling. Consider organizing a yard or garage sale; selling an extra car to simplify life as a one-car household; carpooling to save on gas; limiting eating out and subscription services; selling unused items on Facebook marketplace or Depop; taking on a part-time job; lowering your utility costs by being energy conscious; and utilizing coupons and cashback opportunities when you can. Whatever you do, try to have some fun with it, and remember this is the beginning of something new and positive in your life — not drudgery.

Just a quick tangent on subscription services: these add up quickly, and I often forget how many I have going between music, streaming services, podcasts, audiobooks, and other app subscriptions. Pour through your monthly charges and see what you can cut out. With streaming services, a common practice to save money is just selecting one or two at a time and canceling after a few months when you need a content refresh. Lastly, don't forget to cancel after those free trials. They always get me!

While you're working on your emergency fund, you should **begin** to earnestly create an overall budget for yourself that includes all income and expenses on a monthly basis. If you are unsure how to build a budget, you can either log on to your bank's website, which likely has a budget planning tool you can use for free, or look into other ones available online. There are a lot of free options out there. I would stick to the free ones that keep it simple for now and avoid those that offer a lot of bells and whistles. You're just getting started, don't overcomplicate your new system of money management. You just want a place where you can input your expected income and track everything you spend that is divided into main categories such as rent or mortgage, utilities, grocery, gas, medical, and so on.

Personally speaking, I have a simple spreadsheet with my income and expenses listed on rows that automatically add or subtract when I enter the monthly data. You don't need a complicated paid app subscription or even Microsoft Excel. Google's spreadsheet program, Sheets, is free and can do more than manage your budgeting needs.

Do note that it's recommended you first save up an emergency fund before attempting to pay down any debt other than a mortgage, such as a car loan or credit cards. Regarding personal debt, some people find it easier to start with the smallest debt for a quicker payoff, while others prefer starting with the largest for the greatest satisfaction. I'm not going to go into debt solutions or restructuring as that's not the focus of this particular book, but I will say that a good credit score is important, and reducing personal debt needs to be part of your overall plan. Always opt to pay off the highest interest rates first, as it will save you a lot of money in interest down the road.

If you're more the analog type, just take a piece of lined paper and draw a large capital letter T. Use the whole page. On the left side, list expenses. Keep each bill in its own row and enter your income on the right side. At the bottom, add each side up. Subtract the left from the right, and that number is your available cash flow for the month. A calendar you can write on is particularly helpful when creating a budget if you're the kind of person that likes to physically write these numbers down. If not, use whatever will keep it in your face.

If you have complex debt issues, I recommend that you seek help from either government resources or a highly-rated company specializing in debt management. Some debt management companies provide this service for free. There are also often resources available through the government and nonprofits. I'm not a certified expert in debt management and can only share my personal experiences in hopes they provide some insight and motivation.

As this section comes to a close, I want to say something to you very clearly. Before pursuing any side hustle or business opportunity, it is imperative to have the ability to manage your finances and stick to a budget. This is vital to prevent the likelihood of financial loss, which is particularly hazardous on social media where fraudulent schemes are prevalent.

In any venture, developing the self-discipline to stick to a budget and stay on top of your cash flow is going to set you up for a greater chance at success, regardless of the kind of opportunity. Plus, it helps catch those sneaky subscription fees and gym memberships you forgot about many moons ago.

Building a solid financial foundation allows you to make better choices regarding how you use your money to your own advantage; and not someone else's. I cannot stress to you enough how having a solid understanding of money management is key to your financial success and reducing life's stressors.

Exercise: *Research free or paid resources to help with basic budgeting. Write down at least three. This could include mobile apps, pre-built Excel spreadsheets, or YouTube tutorials.*

Then over the next little while, try out all three and record your experiences with them.

From there, adopt a basic budget for the next month based on what you learned. Spend time discovering more options if you need to do so, but don't use "finding the perfect one" as a reason not to give budgeting a chance. Aim for "good enough."

Think of two to three ways to kick-start your emergency fund. Create this as a short-term goal and make a list of tasks you need to do to achieve it.

Chapter 6:

Self-care is more important

than the other thing.

"You yourself, as much as anybody in the entire universe, deserve your love and affection."

– Buddha

Just like keeping your finances in order, maintaining a healthy lifestyle is also challenging but one well worth the effort. In fact, striving to develop better habits in these areas will make reaching other goals in different areas of our life easier.

Consider the impact of any kind of stress. The healthier you are, the better you can mitigate the impact of stress on your body that comes with running a new business, doing home renovations, and starting a family. If your diet is full of empty calories, you're likely battling low energy and digestive issues, which just creates more hurdles. And we all know the constant stress and anxiety that comes with worrying about any health-related issues and trying to make ends meet.

Neglecting your health and your financial well-being also takes a toll on your relationships with others. When we are worried about big-picture items like money and health, this often spills over into our interactions with others. We're often much more preoccupied with worry, making it difficult to be present and supportive of others. As well, the additional stress leads many to feel more irritable, impatient, or withdrawn — giving rise to more misunderstandings, arguments, and relationship strains.

Self-care plays a vital role in mitigating these big life stressors, but it is also crucial in maintaining your overall well-being. Self-care equips us the necessary tools we need to cope with any kind of challenge that may come up, like learning how to prioritize our own needs.

It also includes learning to set boundaries and acknowledging your pain/trauma. As I'm not a licensed therapist or counselor, I won't go into detail on how to achieve those, especially since there isn't one "right" way that works for everyone. I suggest perusing both local and online professionals to offer help on these topics. As well, there are many online resources available created by professionals in the mental health space that help with this type of work. I strongly recommend taking time to start researching articles from licensed professionals on sites like psychology.com or even take a look at what YouTube, TikTok, and others can offer on the topic from professionals in that space.

That said, I will tell you that setting up proper boundaries allows us to prioritize our own needs, protect our emotional and physical well-being and prevent burnout. The process of learning about and subsequently setting boundaries will stir up a lot of the emotionally charged "stuff" you think you carefully locked away. Not fun stuff. It's never the fun stuff.

Learning to set my own boundaries, hell, even understanding what boundaries looked like, was one of the most difficult and painful processes I've ever gone through. In fact, one of the most pivotal moments in my life would come when I attended a session on boundaries in group therapy for trauma survivors. Little did I know that session would strip the last thin veneer of composure I had left. I could no longer pretend I was fine.

On that day, all my years of a carefully cultivated stiff upper lip, a tightly clenched jaw, and deeply buried emotions were no match for the surging force of suppressed tears ready to surface. They violently collided against the weakened, exhausted fortress I had built around me to survive, exposing long-held scars and veins of vulnerability that threatened the very foundation of the once formidable barrier.

I strained to keep my defenses intact, but the storm within unleashed upon my stoic resolve with the brute strength of a tsunami. The levee could not hold. The unrelenting force — powered by decades of abandonment, profound loneliness, and sorrow — would soon reveal the fragility I desperately sought to conceal.

Moments after the first tear rolled down my cheek, a torrent of emotions would rip through every wall I had spent a lifetime constructing — releasing a deluge of pent-up grief and anguish. The storm's wrath was suffocating, with all the weight of my past coming crashing down in a relentless onslaught of emotional and physical pain.

In those moments, I relived every hurtful word, every betrayal, every raised hand, every shattered hope. I cried for the innocence I never had, for the strength I never should have known, and for the wounds I would always carry.

But, as the tears and agony tore through my body and soul, I also felt its release. I purged my past to make room for a new beginning.

It is only through understanding the depths of our pain that we can find the courage and resilience to rebuild from the wreckage. The pain is temporary, but your growth and resilience will endure past every storm surge.

Boundaries tell people how to love and support us. They promote mutual respect, understanding, and effective communication. For those of us that have lived long periods of life without them, it will provide a different kind of protection. No longer will you need to suffer in silence and sacrifice your own well-being.

When we establish clear limits and communicate our expectations to others, it is **THE ONLY WAY** to maintain healthy relationships and prioritize our own health and happiness.

Please remember that self-care is not selfish, and setting proper boundaries is a vital part of taking care of ourselves and ensuring that we have the energy and resources to live life to the fullest.

Put it down.

I remember when I was struggling with my mental health, everyone just kept getting in my face and sanctimoniously spouting off that I needed more self-care. Which was super annoying and made me feel worse because I didn't really know what self-care was. A bath and a forest soundscape will not fix any of my problems. Plus, I was tired of hearing about the magic of Epsom salts and lavender candles when I was struggling to get through each day and take a shower more than once a week.

But I went on a mission to learn exactly what self-care was to me, and I'm happy to share not only did I discover its power, but I can also share a few ideas I learned along the way. Self-care is different for everyone, but there are some general themes to follow, and overall good advice for most people to jumpstart their self-care routine, such as start sleeping more.

Really, truly. Get a full 7-8 hours of rest a night if you can. I know we often sacrifice sleep to get'r done, but in reality, we're operating at a reduced capacity because our brains and bodies are exhausted. Understandably, this is not always attainable if you have a baby or young child you're a caregiver for someone that keeps irregular hours or needs attention at night. For those that do not have these demands and are burning the midnight oil trying to respond to emails, wasting time on your phone, or even just catching up on housework, this one is for you:

The work will always be there. There will always be something you *need* to get done, but really, all you're doing is creating a system of demands and expectations that normalize self-sacrifice for your job or pile of laundry. You are setting the expectation of torturing yourself.

I'm not saying this is going to be easy or will come without some prickly responses, but you are allowed to create boundaries between work and your personal life. That email can wait until the morning, and it's time to chat with your boss and/or colleagues about maintaining work/life balance and truly clocking out at the end of the day. Burnout is real, and it takes a helluva lot longer to recover from than making someone wait an extra half day on some arbitrary PDF.

As for struggling to go to sleep and stay asleep, the first step is putting your fucking phone down. Put it down. Put. It. Down.

Why? Well, first, the blue light that emits from our smart devices suppresses the production of melatonin, our sleep hormone. On top of that, you are literally using a bunch of lights, colors, sounds, and new information to stimulate and engage your brain — which is the opposite of what you're trying to accomplish. So, see the note above. Put it down. Now leave it. Leeeaaave it.

Beware of big data and its bull shit.

Speaking of getting off your phone, you should do more of that in daylight hours, too — especially social media. Once again, limiting your intake of the constant barrage of the faux life of "look at how great everything is, and how great I am" will help remove added pressure. The comparison game only drives down momentum and drives up feelings of inadequacy.

Now, I know I've knocked social media around quite a bit so far, but I am cherry-picking its drawbacks. We all know the benefits of keeping in touch with friends and family, social impact, saving beloved TV shows, sharing resources, etc., etc., etc. Look, social media doesn't need me to have its back and sell you on it. It's doing fine. But the point of this book is to tell you some direct truths, not lobby in favor of billionaires' tech companies.

However, I wanted to quickly highlight that a lot of online communities exist to provide connection and encouragement in a very real and supportive way without judgement. I have relied on online communities on Reddit after receiving diagnoses of PTSD and ADHD. I was able to learn about people's experiences with certain treatment options, vent, and be validated by a crowd of people that understand what I'm experiencing.

One of my favorite books, *The Body Keeps the Score*, by Dr. Bessel van der Kolk, is full of powerful insights into trauma. One of the points he makes that I consistently use as a guiding light (and as inspiration for this book), is his take on the power of connection. It's connection, not happiness, that is the opposite of trauma — and it's also its cure (van der Kolk, 2014). In whatever way you can connect with someone, including with online communities, that is invaluable and should be used to help bolster your feelings of support. It's just all that other shit.

That other shit being pressures to "keep up" with the highlight reel of people's lives, disingenuous influencers, and lifestyle accounts that portray a constant stream of people who have achieved spiritual awakenings, waterfalls of money, rapid weight loss, 'gained crazy muscles, bro.' You get my drift.

Most of the major social media platforms require that their users disclose if a post is sponsored or not. This is how influencers make the bulk of their income. Companies will pay influencers for a post using their product and will often include a percentage of product sales as part of the compensation. Often this includes an incentive like offering a discount code to entice more buyers. It's not always obvious when you're seeing a sponsored post or advertisement woven into your newsfeed disguised as organic content. Even if you know it's sponsored, it's still going to influence you, as we discussed in Chapter 2.

There's absolutely nothing wrong with doing this; it's the modern-day version of a door-to-door salesperson. Companies can't exist without sales and paying their employees, funding new technology, or business development. We also all have a right to earn an income, and leveraging advertising to do so is not inherently wrong or evil. But it is imperative that you are aware of the social media influence on our spending habits and our feelings about ourselves and how it can make chasing the life you want that much harder.

Seriously, once you click on one type of account featuring a recipe or google something tangentially related to starting a business, you will receive an absolute flood of advertisements, suggested accounts, sponsored posts, events, etc., across platforms.

Why? Because companies like Apple, Amazon, Google, and Facebook have multiple platforms/services/apps, we rely on them to track and share our data. Ever sign up for a random account on an external site that allows you to use your existing Facebook or Google account? Yeah, it's definitely more convenient for the user, but it also provides these major corporations with even more entry points and access to user data.

This is not one of those tinfoil hat conspiracies; this is a well-established privacy concern. Look up the Facebook-Cambridge Data scandal of 2018; they made a documentary about it on Netflix. Anyway, I'm not going to go into "big data"; you can do your own research or ask ChatGPT to explain it to you like a five-year-old (which is extremely helpful for learning complex new things, by the way). The key takeaway here is that these major corporations know way may about you than you think and have an incomprehensible amount of data on human behaviors that their algorithms interpret and turn into the opportunity to sell targeted ad space with fairly spot-fucking-on recommendations.

Combine these incredible data powerhouses with predatory advertising tactics that some industries heavily use — like the online health and wellness industry — you have built a breeding ground for immoral goblins choosing to capitalize on peoples' insecurities about their body image to drive up their annual revenue. Plus, many of these "weight loss cures," growth supplements, and vitamin miracles are not regulated by the FDA (Food & Drug Administration) as drugs but as food. Their promises of quick and effective results may work in the short term but can cause serious harm without any studies documenting or testing their impact on your health/other drug interactions (Dietary Supplements for Weight Loss, 2022).

Always, always, always talk to your doctor and healthcare professionals, like pharmacists, if you start taking a supplement, miracle weight loss tea, start a fad diet, and so forth. First, it's well known that these quick solutions typically result in unsustainable results, but more importantly, because they are not considered "drugs," they are not held to testing standards that medications go through to ensure your safety in both the short– and long-term. This means they can interact with any prescriptions you're on, bring out underlying health issues like high blood pressure, and have not been tested and studied for long-term health effects.

The main point of this section is to once again remind you that there are predatory systems we are exposed to continuously that can truly cause harm, even those that promise to hold all the answers, especially when they promise that.

I am here to remind you that you must do it the hard way. Sorry. The miracles, guaranteed success, overnight cures, healing from all your trauma, growth hacks, make-you-rich products, pitches, books, services, courses — all of it — they just don't fucking work, y'all.

You've got to do the work.

The voice in your head can be a dick.

For most of my life, the absolute toughest critic and most malignant voice criticizing me for my flaws, questioning my capabilities, and making me feel small and insignificant, was my own. This is an all-too-common occurrence. I'm sure many of you are nodding along with me.

There's no one reason why we become our own worst critics; it can be part of our upbringing, perfectionist tendencies, trauma, self-doubt, fear of judgment, and so forth. Whatever the myriad of reasons behind that voice, I'd like to share some advice I received a while back that changed my internal dialogue:

If someone spoke to you the way you speak to yourself, would you want to be their friend?

I can honestly say that was one of the biggest lightbulb moments of my life. Why was I being so cruel and honestly abusive to myself? If anyone else treated me like that, I would sever ties. Keeping a toxic relationship like that only makes me feel worse about myself and negatively impacts every aspect of my life.

Be better to yourself. You are your own advocate.

To be flawed is to be human. No one is perfect in any way. Even in our greatest strengths, there is always room for improvement. Self-development is a lifelong journey. There is literally no upper limit to growth. Even notable figures in sports, business, and media like Serena Williams, Tiger Woods, Bill Gates, Steven Spielberg, and so forth are dedicated to improving their respective games — and publicly preach their never-ending pursuit of personal and professional growth.

Accepting the reality that perfection doesn't exist and all we can be is better than we were the day before is one of the biggest mind shifts that will impact your relationship with yourself and your ability to stay focused on your goals.

Or at least it was for me. That was when I stopped comparing myself to others around me, my circle of friends, and where they were in their lives, careers, bodies, family life, etc. Most of my friends bought houses and obtained career success and more financial freedom (AKA not being super broke) earlier than I did, and I often felt like I was behind in the game of life. But that comparison literally did nothing to serve me or help me reach my goals. In fact, all it did was drive me down further into the shame and depression spiral. The further down I went, the harder it was getting to pick myself back up.

I started consciously evaluating how I was speaking to myself. I even carried a notebook around for a week, and every time I had a negative thought about myself or anything else, I would write down what it was and dig a little into why I was feeling that way.

Reading that at the end of the week was a very eye-opening and, honestly, very rough experience. A clear pattern emerged: I was awful to myself. Even the negative thoughts I had about other things/people really just related back to how I felt about myself. For example, the negative comments I wrote about my boss and our interactions all had some sort of spin about how she thinks I'm stupid, incompetent, hates me, I'm going to get fired, and so forth. Though, to be fair, she was a living fucking nightmare of a human being.

It was so obvious from that point on I needed to improve how I treated myself. It was exhausting and repetitive work. I first started actively interrupting myself every time I started self-criticizing, and then forced myself to say something nice or reframe it to be more neutral. As in, when I was feeling "incompetent," instead of berating myself, I would say aloud,

"I would like to learn how to do this better; where can I get help to learn more?"

When I made mistakes, it was no longer things like "I'm an idiot" or "I'm terrible at this"; it became gentler language like how silly that action was or "my mistake, no biggie." I was given this advice from my therapist, as focusing on the action versus on me as a person allows us to draw a clear boundary between addressing our specific performance vs. whittling away at our self-worth.

Like anything else, it took time to shift my mindset. I very actively and consciously had to correct myself each time (or most times). Additionally, I would go a few steps further with a select number of instances and do a deeper dive inward and reflect on why I was saying these things. With time, these conscious actions would become unconscious and automatic. I had finally started treating myself like the friend I deserved.

Although words alone may not be enough to heal the wounds of trauma, self-esteem, or body image issues, it is still my hope that my words can remind you that you are deserving of a healthy sense of self-worth and that you are not alone in the struggle to obtain it. By focusing on self-love and positive self-talk, we can work toward a more confident and fulfilling life, free from societal pressures, unrealistic beauty standards, and phony clickbait lifestyles.

But remember, it takes time to build new habits, including how to care for yourself. Give yourself a break and realize that even in this, there will be slips and falls. But keep trying. You really are worth it.

Tell 'em to fuck off.

People are judgmental. It's true. You may feel that others are judging you; you have judged others. It happens — also, a fairly universal human experience.

Here's the thing, we often judge people most harshly when we're not feeling right with ourselves, and often about what we're most insecure about. When you're flying high and feeling right with the world, you don't have the emotional time, energy, or fucks to worry about how people are living their lives, how they work, exercise, look, dress, etc.

Most people aren't thinking about you, anyway. Really. We are the main characters of our story, and typically the deep thoughts of the extra in the background working on their laptop or lifting weights at the gym on the movie set are irrelevant to the plot. To most people, we are just that. We're extras. They are not paying attention to you.

The opinions you will get are usually from 2 camps of people: (1) people that matter to you and are there to support you; or (2) they simply do not count because their goal is to tear you and others down to gain a false sense of self-worth. These last ones, yeah, they don't matter, and you can tell them to fuck right off.

Yes, everyone is entitled to their opinion, but you are not obligated to listen to it, give it any weight, respond to it, or even consider it.

Even the opinion of your boss does not necessarily matter. If they're a good leader, it will, but many of us have had toxic bosses that don't offer a healthy environment. That doesn't mean you can be insubordinate. You still need to get paid, but you can do the work without agreeing to their opinion and letting it impact your self-worth, mood, or motivation. It is possible to emotionally detach but still perform.

Know that fear of judgment is a common barrier to making any lifestyle changes. It's a powerful deterrent and creates an environment of insecurity and self-doubt — preventing us from reaching our full potential. You will never be able to please everyone or get everyone to like you or agree with you. Trust me, I tried. It does not work, and you make yourself fucking miserable.

Please know that the more you change for the better, the more you achieve, the higher you go, and the bigger your goals become, the more people will start offering their toxic takes. It has nothing to do with you and everything to do with their own jealousies and insecurities. But at the same time, you become more self-assured and more immune to their malignant behavior.

To the best of your ability, surround yourself with supportive people. That doesn't mean they will blindly take your side, but you know that when they offer feedback, it's done with care, compassion, and what they may think is in your true best interest. You will just have to trust yourself to know when to take that advice and when to follow your gut. Even those with the best of intentions can often project their own insecurities onto you. Trust yourself above all.

Exercise: *Take time to reflect on situations where the fear of judgment stops you from doing something. Whether it was dancing at a wedding, sharing information about your life, or setting/ chasing a goal.*

Write down exactly what it was about their judgment that stopped you from moving forward. How do you feel about that now? Would you still hold yourself back? What would it take for you to try anyway?

Also, think about what things you can start doing to begin your self-care journey.

Chapter 7:

Suck it up, buttercup.

"In three words, I can sum up everything I've learned about life: it goes on."

—Robert Frost.

Work is a necessary part of daily life. While some individuals look forward to their workweek, there are others more ambivalent about it, and there are those that face the Sunday night blues and dread every Monday. I have personally experienced all three of the above.

Regardless of your attitude toward work, it's common to feel dissatisfied at times. Building a fulfilling life takes effort and is full of struggle, even for those who earn high salaries and find themselves at the top of their company, industry, or career field. Nothing will be rosy and wonderful all the time. That's just how life works. We just exchange one set of problems for another.

Keep this in mind as you work towards the life you want, especially if your goals involve starting your own business, switching career fields, or finding a better-suited job. No matter the path you take, it will not be without hardship. Life is not a smooth ride; you will encounter fluctuations in your happiness and resolve no matter where you go and what you do.

I say this not to perpetuate some bleak outlook on life. But to present the reality that if your goal is to live a life of perpetual bliss and happiness, and you base your major decisions on avoiding discomfort, life is going to kick the ever-loving shit out of you.

Struggle and discomfort are inherent aspects of life, especially in the pursuit of meaningful experiences. And it is always worth enduring.

We survive the struggle to appreciate when joy, accomplishment, meaning, and happiness come along. Without the dark, there can be no light. But stick with it, don't see adversity as a sign from the universe to admit defeat. If it's important to you, I once again must recommend the following action: suck it up, buttercup.

This includes having to suck it up and keep your current position while you start getting prepared to make your next move. It's not uncommon to get caught up in the whim and romanticism of the future's promise leading to growing resentment towards your current job or circumstances. Maybe until recently, it's been okay and fine enough to pay the bills, but with the potential of the future feeling almost within reach, this "okay" job has morphed into a soul-sucking experience holding you back.

In times like these, it can often feel that we're trapped in purgatory. We just want to move on with our lives and rid ourselves of this constant push and pull of heightened emotions from the lure of "what could be" to the budding dissatisfaction with our current life setting in like a heavy fog on our hearts. Inside, you're on an emotional roller coaster filled with this sense of urgency that you can't quell.

It's a lot. It is a lot of intense and conflicting emotions that can be both a catalyst for finding the motivation to grind it out and, at the same time, it can also be very emotionally draining. These two things are not mutually exclusive.

It's not abnormal to want to just get on with it either way; it is uncomfortable, to say the least, living in the state of in-between. This discomfort may push you into pulling the trigger either way, quitting your day job to focus all your energy on the next steps. Or just tossing aside the idea as a pipedream or maybe "not the right time" and trying to find ways to settle with where you are right now.

Your dreams cannot happen, growth cannot happen, reaching your potential cannot happen, and meaningful change cannot happen if you don't accept that navigating discomfort is not only inevitable but essential to the process. As is patience and learning to withstand the fear of the unknown. But for those that push through, this is where results happen.

So, in saying all this and before acting on impulse, think about if your current job situation is something that can be endured until you can safely make a switch. If so, I would recommend sticking it out. We've talked about this before, but it's worth mentioning again that the financial stress created by hastily tapping out on one job before there's another to replace it, is a heavy burden.

Let me quickly interject here. Certain situations may necessitate a quick exit, but there are methods to minimize the disruption and make the transitions smooth as possible. That said, no one should ever have to put up with abuse. If you feel threatened, harassed, or abused in any way, this will necessitate some sort of action. Start by talking to a trusted support system regarding the options available to you to mitigate the circumstances.

Back to the matter at hand, ask yourself if you are really prepared to take on the challenge of learning a new business and running it yourself. Be brutally honest because none of those programs from social media ads or your search results will tell you how to do everything, and none of them are as easy as they portray. You still must do all the marketing, banking, legal prep, product research, test samples, website URLs, website design, etc. The to-do list is long. Yes, it changes for each business model, but the list is no less long.

Also, ask yourself, do you have a basic business foundation upon which to draw knowledge to navigate the murky waters of a startup? I'm not trying to discourage you at all—quite the opposite. I'm trying to encourage you to arm yourself with knowledge and, at the same time, provide you with some basic skills you'll need before you sever ties with your steady paycheck. If you do this, really do this, plan a smart transition.

It's necessary to go into any new opportunity with your eyes wide open and armed to the teeth with a profound understanding of what you're getting yourself into. If you don't, you'll risk getting in way over your head. Think your way through your big decisions, don't impulsively feel your way through them.

FOMO and other exploits.

We are absolutely and unequivocally hardwired for human connection. We instinctively seek inclusion in social groups and participation in gatherings, events, and experiences. That very real fear of being left out or left behind is prevalent in each one of us to some degree. It is simply part of the human experience.

I say this because these fears and anxieties relating to the above have received a modern acronym and a place in our daily conversations. FOMO, or the fear of missing out, has so aptly wrapped up this sentiment in a neat and tidy hashtag.

While social media platforms have certainly amplified and accelerated the experience, I wanted to highlight that the feeling itself has its roots in human psychology and social dynamics. But it is often associated with social media and the constant exposure to curated representations of others' lives, which can intensify the fear and perception of being left out or excluded. It can also lead to feeling pressured to make decisions or participate in activities that may not align with what you truly want — contributing to feelings of insecurity, comparison, and the fear of making a wrong choice.

The "happiness hustlers" and so-called lifestyle and business gurus you'll see online use this powerful emotion to exploit for their financial gain, not yours. Using emotionally loaded language like "following your bliss" to evoke that fear you're doing it all wrong, that you are missing out.

First, following your bliss is a very privileged thing to say; not everyone can just jump into a van and travel the world and wake up on a beach and work an hour a day. Also, they probably don't do that. And they often shit in a bucket.

But seriously, following your bliss can very well lead to financial freedom, but it is not without risk. When you have bills to pay, a family to support, and no financial or support safety net, then chasing your dreams becomes a little harder than just selling everything and making a '70s van look impossibly cool inside. It takes patience and making smart, calculated moves that minimize risk where you can.

It's tempting to make happiness the primary objective of your work life, but it can result in disappointment and instability. A more balanced approach that includes other crucial goals, such as financial security and retirement planning, can create a more sustainable and fulfilling career path. Incorporating your income into your budget priorities and focusing on a comprehensive set of goals can help you endure even the toughest work situations.

Remember, you are capable of handling difficult things and can turn a challenging job into an opportunity for growth and personal satisfaction. Take pride in your ability to persist, even if it's just for a little bit longer, as you work toward your bigger goals. Have the courage to keep going and keep fighting to achieve your dream, even if your dream is shitting in a bucket in a remodeled camper van.

Bringing happiness to others at work can also bring happiness to you. Small acts of kindness, like offering a coffee, smiling, or making your workplace more inviting, can positively affect your coworkers and create a more pleasant work atmosphere. Not only can you enhance your own work-life by spreading positivity, but you can also improve the work environment for those around you. Your simple gestures can have a ripple effect and create a more positive experience for yourself and those around you as you push through.

Exercise: *Think of two ways you can make your current work/life environment better for yourself in the short term.*

Then list at least five things you are grateful for right now.

Also, spend a mindful moment appreciating flush toilets.

Chapter 8:

Fortify your mind.

"Content makes poor men rich; discontent makes rich men poor."

–Benjamin Franklin

Suck it up, buttercup — although solid advice — does not give much in terms of actionable steps or tips on how to survive the long endeavor of change ahead of you.

Your mindset will have one of the biggest, if not the biggest, impact on whether you can achieve your goals. There are some tried and true methods that might just make the difference between pushing through or falling short, starting with mindfulness practice.

Mindfulness is not just for the people that shop at crystal stores and burn patchouli incense. There is a plethora of science-backed research on the benefits that mindfulness practices have on our overall well-being — including our ability to persevere.

When we employ methods of mindfulness in our life (which I will get to in a minute), it eventually will help create both a sense of contentment and peace, essential in providing us with balance in every aspect of life. And especially necessary for the high-stakes game of chasing your dreams and slaying them.

Not only will a mindfulness practice reduce stress levels and improve your quality of sleep — leading to better overall health — but it also keeps our mind focused on where we need it. Ever had those nights you can't sleep, and you stare at the ceiling recounting every humiliating thing you've ever done? Or the weird thing you said at a party that got taken out of context? Just me?

Perhaps you've gone on a long road trip down the worst-case scenario highway with no exit in sight. Ruminating obsessively over past regrets and the possible catastrophe around every corner.

Mindfulness trains our minds and bodies to stay in the present, freeing us from these traps and other unnecessary worry and stress. Mindfulness allows us to concentrate more effectively on personal and professional goals, leading to a sense of accomplishment and satisfaction. This doesn't mean ignoring the past and future, but these become considerations of your current life instead of the focal anxiety point.

We cannot change the past, we cannot control the future, and by allowing our minds to stay in the pain of the past or the anxiety of the unknown ahead, we are robbing ourselves of the mental and emotional space of the one thing we can control in this life: how we respond and manage the present.

Be here, right now.

A content mind is one that engages in regular mindfulness practice. It leads to better relationships by facilitating a better ability to connect with others. It also helps to foster a sense of gratitude and appreciation, creating a more positive outlook on life and a greater sense of well-being.

The practice of mindfulness emphasizes being fully present in each moment and nonjudgmentally observing your thoughts and emotions. Let me repeat that last part. **Nonjudgmentally** observing your thoughts and emotions. There are no right or wrong ways to feel about absolutely anything. There is never a way you "should" feel; there is only how you **do** feel. It was a tough learning curve for me to grasp that all feelings and emotions are neutral. There are no "good" or "bad" feelings. They just are.

Mindfulness practice is like any other new skill or activity, and it will take time and patience. Your mind will wander, and you will struggle to break your thought patterns or maintain focus on the present. But harshly judging yourself or self-flagellating for not being "in the moment" just creates an internal dynamic that makes accomplishing this so much harder because of self-criticism and our frustrations with ourselves.

When you catch your mind wandering, it is imperative to just **gently** guide it back to the mindfulness practice without criticism. I found it helpful to picture my mind as a box of ridiculously cute kittens because, at first learning to focus your mind is essentially like herding kittens. How can you get mad at a fuzzy, little baby kitten for just doing what it's naturally inclined to do? You deserve the same soft approach as a tabby cat with little white booties and a pink nose.

To help you get started, I've created a list of my own personal favorite practices, along with a brief description. I encourage you to embrace as many of these practices as possible, as doing so will offer the best results.

Resist the urge to consider any of these as cliché or silly pufferies from new-age yogis that drink really expensive cold-pressed juice with charcoal in it. These are widely accepted mental health practices recommended by the healthcare community:

- **Practice gratitude:** Make a conscious effort to appreciate what you have in your life and focus on the positive aspects of your current situation. This could be as simple as sitting in silence for a minute and listing three things you appreciate each day or writing them in a journal. I personally like to take a pause when I am experiencing feelings of joy, inspiration, connection, and beauty. I consciously breathe in a moment of gratitude that I've been able to create a life to experience and enjoy what's in front of me. In fact, I will share the quote I actively think about in these moments from one of my favorite authors and philosophers, Kurt Vonnegut:

"I urge you to please notice when you are happy and exclaim or murmur or think at some point, 'If this isn't nice, I don't know what is.'"

—*A Man Without A Country*

- **Meditate in a few ways:** I meditate regularly. It is an integral part of my journey to inner peace and directly responsible in part for my growth in self-awareness and my ability to self-align with my core beliefs and desires. I often receive feedback from people that they struggle with meditation because being told when to breathe or sit still ends up feeling stressful for them. Breathwork is just one kind of meditation. I have not always been its biggest fan of it either; I prefer practices that involve scanning how my body feels and actively noticing and releasing tension from one body part to the next. Other meditation practices can include going on walks, repeating mantras, and focusing on feelings of love and compassion. These all can be done with or without the help of guided meditation, dealer's choice. There are plenty of free or paid apps for this and a plethora of YouTube videos at your disposal. Take some time to research different meditation methods and resources; there is not just one way to approach it.

- **Bring mindfulness to everyday activities:** Just pick a short one you do each day, like brushing your teeth, washing dishes, or taking a shower. Focus your attention on the task at hand and fully immerse yourself in it without rushing or being preoccupied with other thoughts. No list planning, worrying about doing something the fastest or most efficient way. Just awareness of your movements and sensations of that activity. That's it.

- **Taking pause:** Throughout the day, stop and smell the roses. Literally smelling roses is great if you have a continuous supply of them, but figuratively this just means taking short mindfulness pauses. Not long — just pause for a moment or two — and bring your awareness to the present. Without judgement, observe your thoughts, emotions, and sensations. A simple acknowledgment of what they are. There is no pressure to analyze, criticize or change them. You are just observing as a neutral party.

- **Observe an object:** Choose an object from your surroundings — anything from a flower to a paper towel. Consider how it looks, observing the colors, shapes, textures, and details. Engage your other senses, such as how it smells, how it feels, or how it sounds when engaging with it. Of course, don't put things in your mouth that shouldn't go there to engage with your sense of taste. You should know better.

The inner peace not-a-checklist.

In addition to mindfulness practices, I also wanted to highlight some other useful life tips that can help you to improve upon your sense of inner calm and contentment — which will ultimately help strengthen your mind and body for the challenging moments that lie ahead. Some of these will be repeated, but their importance bears repeating a thousand times over.

- **Always remember that life is not linear.** Growth of any kind will never just be a straight line up or down; really, nothing in life is. There will always be ups and downs, ebbs and flows, good days and bad. We push through the bad and ride the wave of the good ones.

- **Let go of comparison:** Comparing yourself to others will only lead to feelings of inadequacy and dissatisfaction.

Instead, focus on your own journey and growth. It is you against you only. Are you better than you were yesterday?

- **Embrace uncertainty:** Life is unpredictable, but embracing the unknown can lead to a greater sense of contentment and flexibility in the face of change. We cannot control the future, others, or the world around us. All we can do is embrace the unknown. The only thing we can only control in life is how we respond to it.

- **Develop a growth mindset:** Focus on personal growth and learning. See challenges as opportunities for growth versus signs from the universe to give up or as evidence that the world is pitted against you.

- **Practice self-care:** Taking care of your physical, mental, and emotional well-being will always have a direct impact on how you feel and your ability to handle life's stressors and pressures. Remember, you cannot pour from an empty cup.

- **Build meaningful relationships:** Connecting with others and forming strong, positive relationships can bring a sense of fulfillment and purpose. They also provide necessary support during challenging times.

    "Show me your friends, and I'll show you your future."

    – Dan Pena (2021).

- **Give back:** Helping others and making a positive impact in the world can bring a sense of fulfillment and satisfaction beyond the pressures of achievement and productivity. It helps foster connection with people and causes beyond us, putting stress and challenges in perspective.

- **Set achievable goals:** Having a clear sense of purpose and working towards achievable goals can bring a sense of fulfillment and much-needed focus.

- **Find balance:** Balancing work, leisure, and relationships facilitates our sense of harmony and well-being. Too much of anything, even good things, can lead to burnout and dissatisfaction.

- **Connect with nature:** Spending time in nature is the ultimate stress reliever, mental health booster, cognitive enhancer, exercise motivator, and a reminder that there's a world beyond our trivial daily concerns. It is a reprieve unlike any other. Nature will always find a way to restore your soul and help you fight another day.

- **Celebrate your accomplishments:** Recognize and celebrate your successes and achievements — no matter how small — to acknowledge your growth, improve your feelings of self-worth, and maintain motivation to keep reaching towards bigger goals.

Being flexible is integral in maintaining your sense of inner peace. As we evolve, you will often confront the reality that what once worked well for you may not anymore. Have the courage to let go of the methods, people, things, expectations, desires, or securities you built that no longer serve you or align with this newest version of yourself. You must do so in order to create space for new opportunities and personal growth that lie ahead. But do so with compassion and patience. Saying goodbye to the familiar is no easy feat.

Living a life that brings you contentment, joy, and peace is not something you check off a list. It will evolve as you do. The key to all of this lies within the first word of this paragraph: living. You must take an active part in your life to maintain your momentum and growth. These are lifelong practices, not a crash diet for the soul.

Exercise: *Start cultivating your mindset of inner peace and contentment by selecting at least one of the methods from the above list. Begin your practice today and set a short-term goal of one week to see how it feels. Record your thoughts on the practice. Swap out or add on another method* *for an additional week. At the end of the two weeks, reflect on how they made you feel and if they brought value. Try incorporating for a longer period of time next.*

Then, think about how you feel at your very core. Reflect on the last section and consider what steps you can take toward creating or increasing a sense of peace specific to your life.

Chapter 9:

Crib notes.

There is a lot of information is packed into this short book. But since this isn't a school assignment and there's no final exam, you do not need to worry about recalling everything I've said...though I hope you do. At least the pieces that resonated with you.

Below is a concise summary of the "big lessons" in each chapter we covered in the book. A built-in cheat sheet that I encourage you to use when certain topics start bubbling up for you. Some lessons may take a few reads and a while to set in before it truly clicks.

And that's okay.

Chapter One:

Find your refuge in your passion(s). My love of music ignited my soul and provided an escape from an unhappy childhood. Discovering activities or hobbies that bring you joy and solace can enhance your overall well-being — even in the worst of times.

Prioritize your responsibilities: When I became a mother, I had to make the difficult choice between pursuing my music career and providing a stable life for my daughter. Sometimes, prioritizing your responsibilities and making sacrifices is necessary for the well-being of yourself and your loved ones.

Embrace new opportunities: After leaving the music industry, I pursued a degree in finance and psychology. By doing so, I discovered new interests and new opportunities, leading to personal and professional growth.

Adapt to change: Recognizing when it's time to make a change and stepping out of your comfort zone is crucial for personal growth and happiness. It's also terrifying, but it is the only way we can reach our potential.

Take calculated risks: While risks can be intimidating, sometimes they are necessary to achieve personal and professional growth. Assessing the potential rewards and consequences of risk can help make informed decisions.

Find fulfillment in multiple areas: Life doesn't have to fit into neat boxes, and finding fulfillment in various aspects of life can lead to a more well-rounded and satisfying existence.

Chapter Two:

Social media is mostly bullshit: It promotes the presentation of a curated, idealized version of people's lives, creating a faux veneer of perfection and success.

This can lead to feelings of inadequacy and the belief that everyone else is living a better life.

Social media and digital advertising have a significant impact on our decision-making processes: We are exposed to thousands of ads each day, which encourages a consumer mindset. Many of our decisions are made subconsciously, relying on cognitive biases and associations — making us susceptible to manipulation.

Chapter Three:

Coping mechanisms and crutches are okay: Coping mechanisms help us get through tough times, and it's important to have compassion for ourselves and others who rely on them.

Making healthy changes takes time: Lasting change is challenging and requires perseverance and self-compassion. Don't shame yourself for past habits or behaviors.

Speed doesn't matter; consistency does: Instead of focusing on instant results, prioritize consistent effort towards your goals. Small, incremental progress is still progress. Don't give up; the small steps really do add up.

Time triage and check marks: Actively make time for the things you want to achieve. Evaluate how you spend your days and make space for new habits by cutting back, not eliminating time-wasting activities.

Prioritize and accept imperfections: Learn to prioritize tasks and be okay with imperfections. Consider outsourcing certain tasks to free up time for your priorities.

Use time management tools: Such as productivity apps, creating to-do lists, and setting timers to limit time spent on certain activities.

Remember, change takes time, and it's important to be patient and kind to yourself throughout the process. Give yourself permission to be patient.

Chapter Four:

Setting aside time for activities without tangible outcomes is important: Taking a few minutes each day to get to know yourself, your desires, strengths, and fears can lead to personal growth and improved relationships.

Breaking goals down is essential: Take your time with writing your goals down. Avoid feeling overwhelmed by breaking them into manageable steps. It will help create and maintain momentum. Focusing on immediate steps and researching what it takes to achieve the goal can improve your chances of success.

Pursuing goals requires bravery and vulnerability: It's okay to feel fear and doubt, but showing up and facing them is what matters. Bravery is about acknowledging the struggle and continuing despite the challenges.

Set five realistic short-term goals and two long-term goals. Reward yourself when you achieve them. Goals are a tangible progression of your dreams.

Seeking validation and encouragement from others: Human connection is important, and feeling empowered by people you value helps keep your motivation going. Motivational talks can also boost motivation and inspire action.

Research and follow a professional motivational speaker. Listen to their podcasts, watch their videos, or read their blogs. They often have some great tips and free tools.

Chapter Five:

Managing money wisely: Requires self-discipline and careful planning. Tracking income and expenses, developing ongoing budgeting strategies, and saving enough money is essential for a sustainable lifestyle and preparing for emergencies.

Confront your finances: Daily monitoring of bank accounts and expenses is recommended to develop self-discipline and progress financially in addition to developing a budget.

Sit down and make a simple budget today. Try to stay in your financial lane.

Establishing an emergency fund: This is a crucial step in financial management. The chapter recommends saving at least three to six months' worth of expenses with a short-term goal of $500-$1000.

Chapter Six:

The importance of self-care: The chapter delves into the concept of self-care and provides advice on developing a self-care routine, like disconnecting from your smartphone.

The significance of setting boundaries: Prioritize your needs, protect your emotional and physical well-being, and prevent burnout. Setting boundaries can be challenging and bring painful emotions, but is essential to rebuilding from past traumas, freeing you for growth.

The negative influence of social media on self-perception: Shift your mindset to avoid the pressure to "keep up" with others' lives. Remember, you're only seeing the highlight reel.

Use caution when it comes to products or services promising quick fixes: Do the hard work and avoid relying on miracle solutions or external factors for personal growth and improvement.

Be kinder to yourself: Accept imperfections and focus inward rather than comparing yourself to others. There is transformative power in shifting one's mindset and leading with kindness and understanding. Tend the garden of your mind. Choose the words you describe yourself with care.

Chapter Seven:

Struggles are a part of building a fulfilling life: Regardless of success or high income, everyone faces challenges and dissatisfaction at times. Life involves exchanging one set of problems for another, and effort is required to achieve fulfillment.

Discomfort and hardships are inevitable: Whether pursuing new career paths or starting a business, facing difficulties is unavoidable. Happiness and resolve fluctuate, but pushing through challenges leads to accomplishment and appreciation.

Don't base decisions on avoiding discomfort: Avoid seeking a life of perpetual bliss and making career choices solely to avoid discomfort. Such an approach is unrealistic and can hinder progress.

FOMO and exploitation by "happiness hustlers": The fear of missing out (FOMO) is rooted in human psychology but can be intensified by social media. Beware the lifestyle gurus who exploit FOMO for personal gain, highlighting the need for calculated decisions and risk minimization.

Balance goals: While happiness is important, it should not be the sole objective to always "feel good." A more balanced approach incorporating financial security and retirement planning ensures a sustainable and fulfilling career path.

Happiness is an emotional response to a temporary event. Having a content mind will lead to a more fulfilling life with more moments of happiness.

Chapter Eight:

Developing a strong mindset: Navigate through life's challenges and achieve personal and professional goals. Includes bulleted suggestions on achieving mindfulness as a key practice for cultivating contentment, peace, and focus.

Practical tips for incorporating mindfulness: Tips include practicing gratitude, engaging in various forms of meditation, bringing mindfulness to everyday activities, taking short pauses to observe thoughts and emotions without judgment, and mindfully observing objects in their surroundings.

Strategies to enhance inner peace and well-being: These include recognizing that life is not linear and embracing its ups and downs, letting go of comparisons with others, embracing uncertainty, fostering a growth mindset, practicing self-care, and so forth.

Living a fulfilling and peaceful life is an ongoing process rather than a one-time achievement: It requires active participation, commitment, and the integration of these practices into daily routines.

Lastly, give yourself a break and permission to make mistakes!

Conclusion

Dear Reader,

As we all know, life is full of ups and downs. Having succeeded in accomplishing several goals doesn't mean you are going to have clear sailing from now on. Expect to get bumped around. If you're not, I suggest you're not challenging yourself enough and need to step up your game.

Know that you can power through some of those bumps; other times, you will be knocked so low you might have to start all over again. I know, as it's happened to me more than once. Dust yourself off, straighten your spine, and get back up. Yes, people might talk, but let them. You have more important things to worry about than what other people think about you. You are more important than passing gossip.

Remember that happiness comes to us in part by learning to be content with where we are along the path of our life journey. Please don't misconstrue this as suggesting not to be ambitious or to desire adventure and luxurious things in your life. Being ambitious in life is a wonderful thing that energizes the heart and spirit.

Do make peace with yourself in the knowledge that there is no get-rich-quick method that someone will share with you in their podcast, video course, etc., that doesn't require hard work and usually some sort of financial funding. The old saying, "If it seems too good to be true…" remains annoyingly accurate.

Remember to ask yourself, if someone is making loads and loads of money doing something, why would they share it with you or anyone else unless they profit enough to offset their loss in sharing with you and the rest of the world? Certainly, not all of them are scammers, but it's clear that their presence on social media is solely for the purpose of monetizing their followers. Do your homework. Educate yourself enough to be able to weigh the costs against the benefits. Know bull when you see or hear it.

In closing, I once again encourage you to take active pauses for gratitude and enjoy every small wonder in each of your days. Remember to set realistic short-term goals and stay the course of your pie-in-the-sky, long-term goals. Get organized, stay focused, and be prepared to rise to the occasion, both mentally and physically, when opportunities come your way. Then grab them with both hands and don't look back. And above all, stay true to yourself along the way.

Thank you for reading our book! I wish you all tremendous success in all your endeavors.

You've got this!

–Sara

P.S. If you enjoyed our book, please be so kind as to leave us a review! We'd love to hear from you!

Sign up for our newsletter:

https://www.sarasidwellauthor.com/

Follow us Facebook under our publisher WOXY Press.

Michelle and I will be creating some fun things like bonus content, quizzes, and giveaways. You'll also be notified when our second book on overcoming anxiety, shame spirals, and overwhelming intrusive thoughts is ready for release!

Conclusion Pt. 2

Kind souls,

Although Sara and I are eerily similar in many ways, I do want to offer my own parting words. I echo everything Sara said in the previous section but wanted to add my own twist of lime.

First, it takes a significant amount of bravery and self-awareness to recognize that you want something more out of life than your current circumstances. Taking an action like reading a book (this book!, watching a YouTube video, perusing some online articles, or flipping through mental health TikTok is all an act of self-love and self-care. Not everyone will ever work up the courage to get here because just getting here is hard.

It's uncomfortable to admit when things aren't "quite right," that you need help and that you want more out of life. I know. I lived in denial for a very long time; I was not ready to face my painful realities. I knew long before I received my PTSD diagnosis that I carried more than just the heavy burden of my past. But I wasn't ready to face the darkest recesses of my mind or the wounds etched into my very being.

Once I was ready, I made a promise to myself: to take my time and stop at nothing to heal and create the life I want — on my terms.

I am happier and healthier than I ever thought possible, and I continue to work on moving to a place of thriving vs. feeling just okay-ish. It is a lifelong journey. Each day, I strive to be better than I was yesterday for me.

If I could leave y'all with one last piece of parting wisdom that has made all the difference for me: it is to put kindness and empathy at the center of everything, both in how you treat yourself and others.

It is impossible to know what people are battling. We may think the girl with the big smile and quick wit has it easy, but often those that laugh and smile the most are the ones that have seen the most pain. Your life (and theirs) improves dramatically when you assume the best in people and err on the side of kindness. That one fleeting moment of patience, comfort, and compassion possesses the capacity to provide a shimmer of hope for someone in desperate need. I assure you, it really can make all the difference.

Please remember that showing kindness and practicing empathy is never a sign of weakness. Often, the strongest people are the kindest and most empathetic — because life forced them to be.

For those of us that have felt the constricting, malevolent tendrils of trauma slither through our minds and clamp down on our hearts, we have also confronted the profound depths of humanity's most powerful drive — our unwavering instinct to survive. And because of that, we develop strength and resilience beyond the comprehension of those that have not traversed the harrowing realities of significant trauma.

We understand the magnitude and destructive impact that adversity and struggle set upon the soul. We recognize the complexity of human nature, the pervasive effect our individual actions have on others, the inherent fragility and strength within all of us, and that the experience of suffering is universal.

We see that no matter how seemingly insignificant, our words, choices, and behaviors have the capacity to perpetuate or reduce the pain of others. We know that the smallest act of kindness or the briefest of moments of empathy holds the potential for a ripple effect of healing and inspiration beyond the present.

I draw this distinction to emphasize that it is a logical impossibility that kindness and empathy are a sign of weakness. The strongest, most resilient people that exist have experienced both the depths of depravity and the remarkable compassion of humanity. We serve as a reminder that even in the midst of unfathomable darkness and in the face of the most malignant forces, kindness and empathy will endure — igniting hope, healing, and unyielding courage in all of us.

I'll let Kurt Vonnegut have the final words for me:

"Hello, babies. Welcome to Earth. It's hot in the summer and cold in the winter. It's round and wet and crowded. On the outside, babies, you've got about a hundred years here. **There's only one rule that I know of babies — 'God damn it, you've got to be kind."**

–Michelle

Bonus Section:

With change may come loss.

Loneliness is a common feeling that many people experience when they start working on themselves and pursuing their dreams. This can happen for several reasons, including a lack of support from friends or family, feeling isolated from others who are not on the same path, and feeling overwhelmed by the responsibilities that come with self-improvement and goal setting.

One of the reasons that self-improvement can lead to loneliness is that it often involves letting go of old relationships, habits, and routines. This can be especially challenging when these relationships were once meaningful or served as a source of comfort. For example, a person who decides to give up drinking may find that they no longer have as much in common with their drinking buddies and may feel lonely as a result. Similarly, a person who decides to focus on their career may find that they no longer have the time to socialize as much as they used to. The tug on old familiar bonds can be tempting.

Another reason that self-improvement can lead to loneliness is that it often requires a person to be more self-reliant and independent. While this can be a positive step toward personal growth, it can also mean that a person has less support and companionship from others. This can be especially challenging for those who are used to relying on others for support and guidance. For example, a person who decides to take control of their finances may find that they no longer have someone to turn to for financial advice and can feel pressured to go over budget.

Despite these challenges, it's important to remember that loneliness is a natural part of the growth process. Just as a caterpillar must go through the metamorphosis of becoming a butterfly to fully transform and reach its full potential, so too must individuals who are working on themselves experience feelings of loneliness and isolation along the way.

Remember, these feelings of loneliness are normal and temporary. They will pass as a person continues to grow and develop and subsequently build new relationships that are more aligned with their goals and values. However, there are steps that a person can take to help mitigate these feelings of loneliness as they work on themselves and their dreams.

One such step is to reach out to others who are also pursuing similar goals. This can provide a sense of community and support and can help to mitigate feelings of loneliness. For example, a person who is trying to quit smoking may find comfort in connecting with others who are also trying to quit. Similarly, a person who is pursuing a creative dream may find solace in connecting with others who are also working on similar projects.

Another way to cope with feelings of loneliness is to focus on the positive aspects of self-improvement and pursuing your dreams. Take a person who is working on improving their physical health and may find comfort in the knowledge that you are doing something positive for their well-being. Similarly, a person who is working on a creative project may find joy in the process of creating something new and unique.

Finally, if the feelings of loneliness are too much to bear, it's important to seek support from loved ones or support groups. While it may not always be easy to reach out for help, it's important to remember that support is available. You may be surprised that often a side benefit of reaching out can result in strengthened relationships which can provide a sense of comfort and security during a time of transition.

I'd also like to encourage you not to be afraid of feeling uncomfortable. It is during those times when I've felt so incredibly out of my comfort zone that I've achieved some of my greatest accomplishments. As a reminder to myself, I now have a sticky note on my desk that reads "Stay Out of Your Comfort Zone." Whenever you have those feelings, please resist the temptation to run away from them. Remind yourself that the fastest way out of feeling that way is to take action.

When in need of a source of comfort and encouragement, especially for those of you who are feeling lonely on your journey, I often reflect and connect my journey with nature for a renewed sense of determination. Whether it's the panther stalking solo in the jungle, the jaguar wondering in solitude, or a lion roaming alone, their majesty, beauty, and raw physical power and prowess reflect to me their ability to navigate challenges and obstacles with ease, strength, and grace. Alone.

Connect with the fierce independence that lies within you, and harness it to take on the world with the confidence and conviction you have waiting to be set into the wild.

About the authors.

Sara Sidwell has a BS from Oklahoma State University and has held executive-level positions for over three decades working as a top-tier analyst for a mid-size publicly traded company and as an entrepreneur where she served as the CFO for two thriving startup businesses in the transportation and construction industry. She intimately understands the highs and lows of forging a triumphant career.

When she's not writing, Sara enjoys playing music, hanging out with her family, and vying for couch space with her three English bulldogs and two adopted cats at their home, in South Carolina.

Other works by Sara:

The Happiness Hype, Think Different, Live Different.
10 Things Every Teen Needs to Know –Coming Christmas 2023!

You can find her on **www.sarasidwellauthor.com**

Michelle Riccetto is a marketing executive in the tech industry with a passion for writing and mental health advocacy. She has a BA from the University of Texas in Austin and an MBA from the University of Massachusetts Boston. Her signature dry humor and raw authenticity is evident in both her writing style and in her everyday lived experience. She is known for her unrelenting drive to share her experience as a neurodivergent with ADHD and as a survivor with PTSD in order to reduce stigmas and normalize these important conversations.

She is a self-proclaimed "Oxford Comma Enthusiast" and currently resides in Ottawa, Canada.

You can find her on:

Instagram: @riccetto

Threads: riccetto

LinkedIn: /michellericcetto

If you enjoyed this book and found its contents helpful, please kindly consider leaving us your comments in the review section. We'd love to hear from you!

More books by Sara and Michelle are currently in the works!

References

Aldrich, E. (2019, November 26). I check my bank account daily—And here's why you should, too. The Motley Fool. https://www.fool.com/the-ascent/banks/articles/i-check-my-bank-account-daily-heres-why-you-should-too/

Acharya, S., & Shukla, S. (2012, January 1). Mirror neurons: Enigma of the metaphysical modular brain. Journal of Natural Science, Biology, and Medicine; Medknow. https://doi.org/10.4103/0976-9668.101878

Bridges, F. (2017, July 21). 10 ways to build confidence. Forbes. https://www.forbes.com/sites/francesbridges/2017/07/21/10-ways-to-build-confidence/?sh=39c1edc53c59

Carr, S. (2023, May 10). How Many Ads Do We See a Day in 2023? | Ad Exposure Statistics. Lunio. https://lunio.ai/blog/strategy/how-many-ads-do-we-see-a-day/

Cheevers, C. (2021, February 8). How does sunshine affect your mood? Spectrum News 1. Spectrum News 1. https://spectrumlocalnews.com/nys/central-ny/blog/2021/02/08/how-does-sunshine-affect-your-mood-

Dietary supplements for weight loss. (2022, March 1). Mayo Clinic. https://www.mayoclinic.org/healthy-lifestyle/weight-loss/in-depth/weight-loss/art-20046409

Franklin, B. (n.d.). Benjamin Franklin quote. The Quotable Coach. https://www.thequotablecoach.com/contentm ent-makes-poor-men-rich/

Frost, R (1923, October) "Nothing Gold Can Stay" The Yale Review

GoBankingRates. (2016, May 6). 23 reasons why you'll always be broke. Money. https://money.com/why-you-are-poor/

Graff, F. (2022, August 10). How Many Decisions Do We Make In One Day? PBS North Carolina. https://www.pbsnc.org/blogs/science/how-many-decisions-do-we-make-in-one-day/

Groff, L., & Smoker, P. (1994, December). Spirituality, religion, culture, and peace: Exploring the foundation for inner-outer peace in the twenty- first century. The International Journal of Peace Studies, 1(1). https://www3.gmu.edu/programs/icar/ijps/vol1_1/smoke r.html?gmuw-rd=sm&gmuw- rdm=ht

Grossman, A. (2021, July 24). How spending money to make you feel better doesn't work (Except 2 ways). Frugal Confessions. https://www.frugalconfessions.com/spend-less/spending-money-to-make-you-feel-better/

Growing inequalities, reflecting growing employer power, have generated a productivity–pay gap since 1979: Productivity has grown 3.5 times as much as pay for the typical worker. (n.d.). Economic Policy Institute. https://www.epi.org/blog/growing- inequalities-reflecting-growing-employer-power- have-generated-a-productivity-pay-gap-since- 1979-productivity-has-grown-3-5-times-as-much-as-pay-for-the-typical-worker/

Harvard Health Publishing. (2016, November 9). Trade bad habits for good ones. https://www.health.harvard.edu/staying- healthy/trade-bad-habits-for-good-ones

Haynes, T. (2018, May 1). Dopamine, smartphones & you: A battle for your time. Science in the News— Harvard University.

https://sitn.hms.harvard.edu/flash/2018/dopamine-smartphones-battle-time/

Joi. (2012, January 9). Millions searching: How to be happy. Self Help Daily. https://www.selfhelpdaily.com/how-to-be- happy-3/

Kalish, A. (2020, June 19). You're only making your life harder if you skip breakfast. The Muse. https://www.themuse.com/advice/youre-only-   making-your-life-harder-if-you-skip-breakfast

Karthik K. (2022, January 19). Why is important to think big and aim high to succeed. Motivational Lines. https://motivationallines.com/why-it-is-   important-to-think-big-and-aim-high-to- succeed/

Laja, P. (2022, December 16). First Impressions Matter: Why Great Visual Design Is Essential. CXL. https://cxl.com/blog/first-impressions-matter-the-importance-of-great-visual-design/#:~:text=People%20make%20snap%20 judgments.,they'll%20stay%20or%20leave.

Lohr, J. (2015, May 1). Can visualizing your body doing something help you learn to do it better? Scientific American Mind, 26(3), 72–72. https://doi.org/10.1038/scientificamericanmin d0515-72a

Maranjian, S. (2019, July 28). 15 downsides to being rich. The Motley Fool. https://www.fool.com/retirement/2019/07/28/15-downsides-to-being-rich.aspx

McLean Hospital | Here's How Social Media Affects Your Mental Health | (2023, January 18). https://www.mcleanhospital.org/essential/it-or-not-social-medias-affecting-your-mental- health

Morse, G. (2014, August 1). Hidden Minds. Harvard Business Review. https://hbr.org/2002/06/hidden-minds

Motivation: How to get started and stay motivated. (2022, October 19). Healthdirect Australia. https://www.healthdirect.gov.au/motivation- how-to-get-started-and-staying-motivated

Myers, C. (2018, October 20). If you want to achieve long-term happiness, embrace the growth mindset. Forbes. https://www.forbes.com/sites/chrismyers/201 8/10/20/if-you-want-to-achieve-long-term- happiness-embrace-the-growth-mindset/

Nicola, S. (2021, August 24). How to foster gratitude. WebMD. Retrieved February 6, 2023, from https://www.webmd.com/balance/features/gr atitute-health-boost

On the Link Between Great Thinking and Obsessive Walking. (2021, August 23). LiteraryHub. https://lithub.com/on-the-link-between-great- thinking-and-obsessive-walking/

Patel, N. (2020, January 24). Infographic: How Colors Affect Conversions. Neil Patel. https://neilpatel.com/blog/how-colors-affect-conversions/

Pena, D. (2021, November 11). Show me your friends and I'll show you your future. DX Innovation Institute. https://dxinnovationinstitute.com/show-me- your-friends-and-ill-show-you-your-future/

Pentis, A., & Giovanetti, E. (2021, September 30). Should you build an emergency fund or pay off debt? LendingTree. https://www.lendingtree.com/debt-consolidation/emergency-fund-or-pay-off- debt/

Poow, C. (2020, December 18). Bass line: What is a bass line in music & how do I write one? Music Gateway. https://www.musicgateway.com/blog/how- to/write-a-bass-line

Ramsey Solutions. (2023). A proven plan for financial success. https://www.ramseysolutions.com/

Riopel, L. (2019, June 14). The importance, benefits, and value of goal setting. PositivePsychology.com. https://positivepsychology.com/benefits-goal- setting/

Robson, D. (2017, August 28). The amazing fertility of the older mind. BBC Future. https://www.bbc.com/future/article/20170828-the-amazing-fertility-of-the-older-mind

Seppälä, E. (2017, May 8). Proof That Positive Work Cultures Are More Productive. Harvard Business Review. https://hbr.org/2015/12/proof-that- positive-work-cultures-are-more-productive

Smith, M. (2022, December 6). Cultivating happiness. HelpGuide. https://www.helpguide.org/articles/mental-health/cultivating-happiness.htm

Snowden, R. (1986, December 1). Gambling times guide to bingo. Lyle Stuart. https://www.amazon.com/Gambling-Times- Guide-Bingo-Snowden/dp/089746057X

Subramaniam, A. (2021, October 22). What quitting social media taught me. Psychology Today. https://www.psychologytoday.com/us/blog/p arenting-neuroscience- perspective/202110/what-quitting-social-media-taught-me

Szalavitz, M. (2017, January 1). Dopamine: The currency of desire. Scientific American Mind, 28(1), 48–53. https://doi.org/10.1038/scientificamericanmin d0117-48

Taibbi, C. (2012, November 4). Brain basics, part one: The power of visualization. Psychology Today. https://www.psychologytoday.com/us/blog/gifted-ed-guru/201211/brain-basics-part-one-the- power-visualization

Time management app. (2017). Clockify. https://clockify.me/time-management-app

Top 10 best free time management apps in 2023. (2023, February 1). Software Testing Help. https://www.softwaretestinghelp.com/time- management-apps/

Truth behind weight loss ads, The. (2022, August 17). Federal Trade Commission Consumer Advice. https://consumer.ftc.gov/articles/truth- behind-weight-loss-ads

van der Kolk, B. A. (2014). The body keeps the score: Brain, mind, and body in the healing of trauma. Viking.

Van Edwards, V. (2022, October 7). 21 tips on the psychology of advertising to maximize sales. Science of People. https://www.scienceofpeople.com/body- language-advertising/

Van Praet, D. (2014, October 30). How your brain forces you to watch ads. Psychology Today. https://www.psychologytoday.com/us/blog/u nconscious-branding/201410/how-your-brain- forces-you-watch-ads

Weinschenk, S. (2015, October 22). Shopping, dopamine, and anticipation. Psychology Today. https://www.psychologytoday.com/us/blog/brain-wise/201510/shopping-dopamine-and- anticipation

www.ingramcontent.com/pod-product-compliance
Lightning Source LLC
LaVergne TN
LVHW051350080426
835509LV00020BA/3378